NOT
IN
OUR
SCHOOLS?!!!

SCHOOL BOOK CENSORSHIP IN CANADA
A DISCUSSION GUIDE

Judith Dick

1982

CANADIAN LIBRARY ASSOCIATION

Canadian Cataloguing in Publication Data
Dick, Judith
    Not in our schools?!!!

ISBN 0-88802-162-3

1. Text-books--Canada--Censorship. I. Canadian
Library Association. II. Title.

LB3048.C3D52   379.1'56   C82-090064-8

Published by The Canadian Library Association
151 Sparks Street, Ottawa, Ontario K1P 5E3
Copyright 1982 The Canadian Library Association
ISBN 0-88802-162-3

Printed and bound in Canada

CONTENTS

Censor: an officer or official charged with
scrutinizing communications to
intercept,
suppress,
or delete
materials harmful to his country's
or organization's interests...
one who lacking official sanction but
acting ostensibly in society's interests
scrutinizes communications, compositions,
and entertainments to discover anything
immoral,
profane,
seditious,
heretical,
or otherwise offensive.

Webster's Third
International Dictionary

Finally, brethren,
whatever is true,
whatever is honorable,
whatever is right,
whatever is pure,
whatever is lovely,
whatever is of good repute,
if there is any excellence, and
if anything worthy of praise,
let your mind dwell on these things.

The Bible
Philippians 4 : 8

Introduction

In 1974, the day the USSR was forcing Solzhenitsyn
into exile, the Nova Scotia Department of Education removed *One Day in the Life of Ivan
Denisovich* from its approved list. (11)

The escalating number of news stories about schools and
controversial materials, the proliferation of articles on the subject in
recent journals, the formation of vocal "pro-banning" and "anti-
banning" pressure groups all indicate that the subject of censorship in
our schools is much on people's minds and therefore deserves serious
consideration. This book is intended as a readable, informative,
general guide for parents, teachers, administrators and others who
are becoming increasingly concerned about the choice of school
books in Canada. At present, there is no one publication that
performs this function within the context of Canadian education,
although educators have ample access to information from the
United States. It is most important, therefore, that the specific issues
involving censorship in Canada be outlined, to avoid misconceptions
created by deducing from the American context. This book has
attempted to present a national picture, although it must be admitted
that the focus is primarily on English Canada.

The approach to censorship taken has been very broad. It includes
the kind of censorship whereby books chosen by professionals for
inclusion in the classroom are challenged by members of the
community on moral or other grounds; but it also includes the kind of
censorship that may occur when one book is chosen over another.
Books should be chosen for their strengths rather than rejected for
their weaknesses. When weaknesses are over-emphasized or when
books are devalued because of the potential for controversy, censorship can occur. Bias in the selection and writing of educational

materials is also an important factor, since many groups consider themselves to be unrepresented or unfairly represented in our educational system.

Broad, too, is the scope of this work in dealing with "books in schools". This wide sweep has been dictated by the necessity of relying on sources such as newspaper reports, which rarely distinguish bona fide textbooks from books held in school libraries or trade books approved for use in a particular course. Consequently, in this study, educational books have at times been dealt with as a whole and not classified according to whether they are recommended trade books, library books or textbooks.

A broad variety of episodes concerning controversial books in Canadian schools have been cited or described. Although controversies over religious instruction, films, and family life programs are not discussed, many of the same factors are involved. To illustrate various types of incidents, a number of articles have been reprinted throughout the book. Following many of the articles are lists of questions entitled "Something to think about." These questions are intended to generate analysis and discussion of some of the more difficult issues involved in censorship controversies. Often there is no clear-cut "correct" answer. It is hoped that the questions will lead the reader to examine various aspects of the problems and to think about the issues seriously.

The sources of information about school book controversies are chiefly newspaper and journal articles. No word-of-mouth experiences are included. There are, however, some limitations in relying on press coverage for research. These include the lack of indexing for certain newspapers, the absence of follow-up stories, errors or omissions in reporting, and the seemingly random choice of stories. Reports are often inconsistent and their publication may depend upon whether or not space is available in the newspaper or upon the attitude of a particular editor or reporter to a story involving censorship. Other news items may pre-empt a story about a local school conflict. Furthermore, conflicts occurring in small communities where news coverage is limited may not be reported at all. The large proportion of stories from Manitoba do not indicate a disproportionately high number of censorship conflicts in that province but only reflect the availability of source material to the author, a Manitoba resident. These limitations notwithstanding, newspapers and journals remain one of the most important sources of information and have provided the starting point for the research involved in producing this book.

In order to respond constructively to the issue of censorship in Canadian schools, one must approach the topic from a broad variety of perspectives. Problems of controversial materials and censorship in Canadian schools will be placed within the context of the history of school book selection practices; the "offensive" elements of school books will be examined; the sources of complaints will be discussed; and the judgements and results of various school book conflicts will be presented. With a knowledge of various incidents involving controversial materials in schools, the potential for rational discussion and positive action may be increased. The final chapter addresses itself to ways in which we, as parents, educators, or concerned citizens might deal with problems in this area.

I. How Are School Books Chosen?
A Brief History

It is enlightening to glance back at the history of procedures in the selection of school books in Canada. The report of Lord Durham on conditions in Upper Canada following the Rebellion of 1837 stressed the importance of finding suitable texts for schools, either by importing them from England or by compiling and printing them in Canada, presumably to prevent United States republican ink from seeping into young Canadian brains. Egerton Ryerson was appointed Superintendent of Education for Upper Canada in 1844 and for over 30 years he influenced the development of public education in what was to become Ontario. A Methodist minister, he emphasized the teaching of biblical history and morality, natural history and philosophy, civil government and political economy, in addition to the three R's and other subjects. Despite the fact that he deplored American republicanism, Ryerson was the prime mover in changing the then-prevailing concept of education for only the upper class of Canadians: he called for a system of universal education and worked to implement it. The School Act of 1846 provided for provincial boards of education, whose duties were to provide a normal school for teacher training, to recommend textbooks, and to establish controls for common schools. The act provided for the super-intendent "to discourage the use of unsuitable and improper books in the schools, or school libraries, and ... to provide for and recommend the use of uniform and approved textbooks in the schools." Thus began the system of authorized texts; authority was maintained by a grants scheme, and schools had to conform to certain regulations in order to obtain grants for the purchase of school books. A single series of textbooks was adopted for public schools, and Canadian publishers printed them. By 1888 the annual list of authorizations had become known as Circular 14 in Ontario. These annual circulars are still issued by provincial departments of education.*

In 1907 the question of textbooks arose again: it seems they had "fallen behind the times". A separate office in each department of education was created to handle textbooks; the principle was still to authorize locally prepared texts, rather than British or American imports. If Canadian texts were unavailable, a British text could be chosen providing it did not do violence to the Canadian spirit; *no* American text, according to policy, could be chosen.

After the First World War, at a time known to educators as the utilitarian period, scientific research began to acquire new prominence. However, during the 1930s a new philosophy took hold. John Dewey, an American, argued about such things as the nature of a child and the importance of an encouraging environment for development of natural inquisitiveness. Dewey's philosophy had a strong appeal for most educators. It also had strong implications, for between 1928 and 1937 an extensive revision of the curriculum was carried out in every province in Canada. Generally, the system for selection of texts changed little: books were not so much prepared under department of education direction as "let out to tender". Committees were created to select textbooks, and on notification of a need for a particular book, publishers would submit one for consideration. The selection committee would supervise alterations or revisions. Occasionally, an American book was chosen.

The real change in the system of adopting books for schools came in the 1950s and early 1960s with the move from authorized to approved textbooks (128). The British system of single texts prescribed by the provincial departments of curriculum to be used in all classrooms was abandoned in favour of a structure modelled along the lines of that prevalent in the United States. American influence in education, as in most sectors, outstripped that of the old European countries following the Second World War. This model decentralized curriculum decision-making, giving the individual teacher greater responsibility. Canadian educators were offered a choice of textbooks approved by provincial departments of education, and "stimulation grants" tied to the old system of authorization and specifically allocated to the purchase of textbooks were terminated.

---

* *This short history concentrates on Ontario since that province, with its early settlement and growth pattern, and its large population, has housed most of the textbook publishing industry. Many publishers are now regionally based and could produce their own histories.*

The general effect of this process was to open up the educational market for books into a kind of "free market" system. Circular 14 in Ontario, for instance, has grown to approximately 100 pages of lists of department-approved texts. The difficulty of choosing from what is essentially a computer print-out of book titles has been pointed out by Paul Robinson in his exhaustive study of textbooks in the Atlantic provinces (156). Moreover, responsibility for choosing texts has fallen to individual teachers, department heads or school principals, on the basis of the choice offered to them. For example, titles to be used in English literature courses are not listed in Circular 14. In Ontario, English literature titles to be studied are chosen by principals and teachers with approval by school board resolution (123).

In some other provinces, the department of education approves lists of recommended titles although final approval rests with the school boards. Regardless of how English literature titles are chosen, they are not usually "textbooks" intended for student use, but are trade books. For example, novels such as *Flowers for Algernon, Who has Seen the Wind?* and *One Day in the Life of Ivan Denisovich* are trade books, which might be approved for use in an English course in order to teach theme, characterization, style, etc. The question of censorship can arise when decisions are made to alter these trade books for student use.

In choosing textbooks, other factors become important. Given the larger promotional efforts of American educational publishers and their ability to modify texts developed in the United States to satisfy Canadian requirements for inclusion in approved lists, while keeping costs down,* the ability of Canadian publishers to forecast the educational market and compete in sales of books in terms of numbers and prices has been seriously affected. In 1965, the Hall-Dennis Report, *Living and Learning,* proclaimed "undue American influence" in books in Ontario schools. The demise of two traditional textbook producers who developed texts here for Canadian needs may have underlined the impact of the "American influence": The Ryerson Press was bought out by a large American textbook producer and is now part of McGraw-Hill Ryerson, and Gage Publishing was taken over by Scott Foresman of Chicago. These transactions led to a 1970 Ontario Royal Commission on Canadian Publishers and Publishing.

---

* *Most departments of education make no distinction between original texts developed and produced in Canada and 'Canadianized' versions of U.S. texts adjusted for the Canadian market and produced here by branches of the parent firm.*

These changes have had immense repercussions in the censorship debate, for the basis on which books are chosen is not at all clear in a system so decentralized. Often, as John Wilkinson points out in his excellent study, *Canadian Juvenile Fiction and the Library Market,* the grounds for choosing school books may be "largely rudimentary." (160) Then, too, the lines of responsibility once a book is challenged are not clear; a book which is on a department of education approved list may be challenged within a local school board area, and the easiest way of dealing with the controversy may be to remove it from a school's shelf and make it available only on request.

The inclusion of trade books on curriculum lists, the explosion of the book publishing industry and the "liberalism" of the late sixties have made more potentially controversial materials available to schools. Also increased government spending on education in the sixties and seventies allowed for the purchase of more school materials, thereby increasing the possibility of schools acquiring some of the more controversial books. Current selection practices do allow for a certain amount of flexibility in choice, but in the eighties, with current budget cutbacks, the danger of buying books on the basis of price, rather than quality or educational needs, certainly exists. Obviously there are many factors relating to current selection practices and the context in which selections are made that mesh with the tensions over school books that some communities now face.

II. What Aspects of School Materials Are Offensive?

The definition at the beginning of this study indicates that the censor scrutinizes material for anything "immoral, profane, seditious, heretical, or otherwise offensive." Specific cases of books in Canadian schools being challenged on each of these counts are numerous. Other aspects of school materials are also criticized. This chapter presents various types of complaints that have arisen in the past. In some of these instances, the books have been removed from schools, in others, they have remained. This chapter will centre on those aspects of school books which have been considered "offensive".

A. Immoral Aspects

Nowadays, when the word "immorality" is mentioned, it is generally taken to mean sexual immorality. Moreover, many people seem to regard any treatment of sexuality as immoral. One Canadian survey (122) revealed that books with sexual themes are most likely to arouse parental objection. Furthermore, it seems that the subject matter rather than its treatment causes concern. According to the survey, librarians feel that parents will object to materials on the basis of what they can see at first glance. The practice of marketing books by placing suggestive but frequently misleading illustrations on the front cover or by using provocative titles would seem to make certain books prime targets for criticism. Interestingly enough, Fasick and England (122) point out that the increased interest in censorship has tended to make younger librarians more cautious than their older counterparts in ordering certain books. Some school board deliberations on books are now tending towards open hearing as school materials become a matter of public controversy attracting considerable attention. For individuals working under "enlightened" school boards, it may be a case of "little to fear but fear itself" when it comes to public debate, as illustrated by the following episode.

In February 1976 *The Diviners*, which had been approved for Grade 12 study, was suspended by the principal of Lakeside (Ontario) High School, who apparently acted upon receiving complaints from parents. A twelve-member Textbook Review Committee was set up, composed of two school trustees, two teachers, two clergymen, and six taxpayers. Despite a heavy campaign led by Pentecostal church members, which garnered a 4300-name petition to have *The Diviners* removed, the book was approved for study by the committee and by the board. It was no doubt the actions of one individual, the head of the English department of the high school, "to press for a full public hearing" (4), when an approved book was removed that helped to bring the problem out into the open and assure proper channels were set up for its resolution. This is not to say that the issue did not polarize the community, but it did indicate that there was support for the book as well as criticism of it.

Other examples of books being challenged on the basis of advocating immorality, specifically books with explicit sexual references, can readily be found. The school board of Cranbrook, British Columbia, banned *Flowers for Algernon,* which was being used as part of the Grade 9 curriculum, following one parent's claim that it was "filthy and immoral" (138, p. 37). This award-winning novel was a supplementary textbook on the British Columbia Department of Education list of approved books for Grade 9, and was recommended for Grades 9 and 10 by the 644-member British Columbia Secondary Association of Teachers of English. After the parent complained, it was removed from the curriculum and from the school library. One month later, school board trustees reconsidered, and the book was returned to the school library. However, in Cranbrook, it no longer formed part of the Grade 9 curriculum (5).

At a St. Boniface School Board meeting in Winnipeg, several parents withdrew angrily after raising a number of complaints. One of these concerned the anthology *Winnipeg Stories* which included a story of a young couple who have premarital sex (101). The book is on the Manitoba Department of Education approved list for Grade 11.

Halton, Ontario parents protested against the use of *Go Ask Alice* in English courses. The book, centring on a teenage girl's experiences with sex and drugs, is the diary of the girl's unsuccessful struggle to escape the drug scene. In this case, the trustees resisted the parents' demands (98).

A Richmond, B.C. school board decided to remove the same book from secondary school libraries and send it to the public library. Students were outraged and presented a petition to the school board. The Richmond Teacher-Librarians' Association supported the petition. One seventeen-year-old Richmond student pointed out that banning the book encouraged people to read it. This proved to be true: Richmond bookstores quickly sold out of this title (32).

The Langley, B.C. School Board followed the lead of its Richmond counterpart. Although an *ad hoc* committee of school librarians, parents and trustees recommended that the book be removed from school libraries to counsellors' offices to be used when suitable, the school board decided to remove it from the school entirely (55).

In St. Vital, Manitoba, art books depicting nudity were objected to by a parent. The principal tore the offensive pages from the book. The librarian wondered where an art book without nudes could be found and questioned the usefulness of a book with pages missing.

The article by Drabble (Figure 1), cites two incidents where the centre of controversy was *The Diviners,* by Canadian author Margaret Laurence. The source of contention was the perceived immorality in the book.

Figure 1:

PASTOR PROTESTS 'IMMORAL' BOOK

By John Drabble
Tribune Staff Writer

A Winnipeg pastor wants The Diviners, a critically acclaimed novel by author Margaret Laurence, removed from a Winnipeg high school literature course, saying the book is immoral.

Dan Dugan, pastor of St. Vital Community Fellowship, said he protested use of the book in school courses because it contains certain passages dealing with sex.

"Everyone should be free to buy the book, but I don't think it should be subjected on a captive audience of high school students," he said.

Mr. Dugan said the novel is part of a Grade 12 literature course at

Grant Park High and perhaps at other schools too.

"All I want is parents to look into books their children are reading," he said.

Mr. Dugan conceded he has not read the novel thoroughly, but said his main concern is with certain passages which describe sexual encounters between two characters.

He cited five pages in the 382-page novel which contain passages he considers objectionable, plus some profane dialogue.

However, Grant Park High principal Irvin Sera said Mr. Dugan so far has not laid any complaint with the school's advisory committee, a group of parents, teachers and students that deals with all school matters.

In fact, he said, "neither me nor my predecessor has ever received a complaint about a book used in the high school."

Mr. Sera questioned why Mr. Dugan is complaining about use of the book in the school when he is not a member of the community surrounding Grant Park High.

When published in 1974, The Diviners was hailed by critics as a major artistic achievement. It also received the Governor General's Award for Fiction.

But two years later the book became the target of a Peterborough, Ontario, citizens group that demanded it be struck from the curriculum for Grade 13 students at a Lakefield, Ontario, high school.

The 17-member Peterborough school board voted to keep the book, despite a number of delegations and a 4,300 name petition.

Peterborough school superintendent Rae Linton said in an interview the board feels it made the right decision.

Almost all of the board's members have been re-elected since the dispute over the book in 1976. Moreover, none of the candidates who ran for school board on a platform opposing the novel won office, he said.

Mr. Dugan said he does not intend to launch a similar campaign against the book in Winnipeg. But he has written letters about it to his local St. Vital's School Board (which does not use the book), a community newspaper and to Renaissance Manitoba, a group which opposes sex education in the schools.

Margaret Laurence, who grew up in Neepawa, settled several years ago in Lakefield, Ontario, where she watched with dismay the controversy over her novel.

Two of her other novels are on the department of education's list of approved texts. The Diviners is not on the list, but a department spokesman said it could still be taught in Manitoba classrooms at the discretion of the teacher.

Jerry Dorfman, head of Kelvin High's English department, says he does not use The Diviners in his classes. "But offhand, I see no reason why it couldn't be used.

"There is no question," he said, "that Margaret Laurence is one of the outstanding figures in Canadian literature."

Mr. Dugan said he decided to protest use of the book after reading a statement by Manitoba Teachers' Society general-secretary

Bob Gordon, published in the South East Lance.

Mr. Gordon said in the community paper that school officials rather than parents must make decisions in areas such as placement of children in class, student evaluation and teaching methods.

But Mr. Dugan argued that use of The Diviners in schools is one example of why parents should become involved in what happens at their children's school.

Reprinted from the WINNIPEG TRIBUNE, Feb. 3, 1978, p.3.

Figure 1: Something to think about

1. Do books that contain references to sexuality belong on the Grade 12 curriculum if they meet educational objectives? On the Grade 9 curriculum?
2. The pastor cited snippets from the book to support his viewpoint; however, he admitted he had not read the book thoroughly. Is it important to read sections of the book in the context of the whole in order to judge morality?
3. Is it significant that the pastor is not a member of the community to whom he is addressing his complaints?
4. Is the statement attributed to the general-secretary of the Manitoba Teachers' Society, that "school officials rather than parents must make decisions ..." a provocative one? A legitimate one? Why or why not?
5. Consider the pastor's statement that "the use of *The Diviners* is one example of why parents should become involved in what happens at their children's school". Is this statement valid?
6. What are the rights of the 4300 Peterborough parents who signed the petition in favour of banning *The Diviners?*
7. Why is sexual immorality in books more offensive than other kinds of immorality? Is the exposure of children to other kinds of immorality objectionable? Is there a difference? Why or why not?

B. Profane Aspects

Frequently, school books are challenged because their language is considered to be profane. Conflicts over language may stem from basic differences between fundamentalist Christianity and modern liberalism. Yet it would be misleading to say that the controversy over language is merely one of a religious approach versus a secular approach. The Virden, Manitoba, situation shows that there are differing opinions within the church community itself concerning the principle of censorship. The controversy in Virden was sparked by a series of meetings led by Rev. Ken Campbell, founder and president of Renaissance International, and focused on the language of a number of school books. These included *To Kill a Mockingbird, One Day in the Life of Ivan Denisovich, All Quiet on the Western Front, Brave New World, 1984, Who Has Seen the Wind* and *More Joy in Heaven*, all approved for school use by a committee of teachers, trustees, parents and superintendents between 1972 and 1975 (83).

A minister in Virden took up the pro-banning position, but another minister, who opposed the banning, defended the school board as well as the books in question and organized a public meeting. The issue was further brought to a public forum when the minister promoting removal of the books used banning as his platform in school board elections. He was not elected. However, one book, *One Day in the Life of Ivan Denisovich* was replaced by *Fahrenheit 451.* The split in the community caused deep wounds which remained even after the specific issue was superficially resolved (35, 37, 38, 39, 67, 75, see also Figure 4).

An incident involving the language in a book for younger children arose in Hamilton, Ontario. Edith Fowke's book *Sally Go Round The Sun* was withdrawn from a public school library after one parent complained about the language. One of the verses in question was:

Helen had a steamboat. The steamboat had a bell.
Helen went to heaven. The steamboat went to ...*
Hello Operator! Just give me number nine.
If the line is busy, I'll kick you up ...
Behind the Iron Curtain there was a piece of glass.
Helen stepped upon it and hurt her little ...
Ask me no more questions, tell me no more lies.
That is the whole story of Helen and her lies.

From SALLY GO ROUND THE SUN by Edith Fowke, 1969, reprinted by permission of The Canadian Publishers, McClelland and Stewart Limited, Toronto.

Fowke, a renowned collector of folklore, had won the 1969 Canadian Library Association Book of the Year Award and a silver medal in Leipzig in 1971. She commented, "It would be a misrepresentation of children's lore to [omit] any of the slightly naughty verses in which children take delight" (26).

In Brandon, Manitoba, a parent complained about the "gutter language" used in the story "Debut" included in *Impact*, a short story

---

* *The ellipses are part of the verses. The offensive words do not actually appear in print.*

13

anthology approved by the Manitoba Department of Education for use in the Grade 10 curriculum. In Waskada Secondary School, Brandon, the book was being taught in Grade 9 classrooms. More complaints about the book surfaced after a letter appeared in the local papers quoting the offensive passages. The removal of the offending story was the result. The book was physically taken apart and "Debut" was removed. Other stories from the book remained available for use by students and teachers (105).

The taking up of extreme positions has the potential of exciting emotions and damaging community relations far beyond the damage alleged to be caused by a school book. It is important for everyone involved to read the book in its entirety before assuming a position. Trustees of the Grey County Board of Education in Ontario voted to ban three novels accused of containing profanity and vulgar language, despite the fact that a number of the trustees had not read them. When they later read the books, several trustees regretted voting in favour of the ban. The details of this situation are outlined in Figure 2.

Figure 2:

Trustees change their opinion after they read banned books

by Howard Fluxgold

Trustees for the Grey County Board of Education in Central Ontario have banned three books from regular use in their schools because they believe they are obscene, even though one of the trustees who proposed the move had not read any of the books and has since changed her mind.

The trustees voted 8-6 in favor of the ban.

The books are: The Last Canadian, by William Heine, editor of the London Free Press; My Shadow Ran Fast, an autobiography by Bill Sands, a former cellmate of executed murderer Caryl Chessman at San Quentin prison; and Viva Chicano by Frank Bonham.

Barbara Taylor, one of the trustees who proposed the ban at a board meeting about two weeks ago, said in an interview on Monday that she objected to the "profanity and vulgar language" in the books.

Mrs. Taylor, a mother of four, said she had not read any of the books, but helped instigate the ban because two other trustees, Ward Agnew and Peter Hillyer, "had expressed concerns. I have complete confidence in what they have to say."

However, in an interview yesterday, Mrs. Taylor said that since the vote she had finished reading two of the three books and now is "not happy" with her decision. "I think they're good books. I don't know what my next course of action is," she said.

Another trustee, Helen Johnstone, also said she regretted voting against the books. Mrs. Johnstone said she took the word of others who spoke against the book at the board meeting. She said she has since read the books and "couldn't get over what we've done."

The books were proposed by Arthur Knechtel, an English teacher at Owen Sound Collegiate and Vocational Institute. Mr. Knechtel said he wanted them for use for students in occupational classes.

My Shadow is a convict's description of his rehabilitation, while Viva Chicano tells the story of a youth falsely accused of murder. The Last Canadian is an adventure story dealing with nuclear disaster.

Mr. Hillyer, who also moved to ban the books, said in an interview that the books were "secularist books which have no reference to God .... Parents look to us (trustees) to protect and uphold the values they protect at home."

From "Trustees change their opinion after they read banned books" by Howard Fluxgold, GLOBE AND MAIL, June 12, 1980, p.5, reprinted by permission of THE GLOBE AND MAIL, Toronto.

Figure 2: Something to think about

1. Why is it important that school materials be read before action is taken and before public statements are made? Is relying on the opinions of other people advisable?
2. How could the trustees have handled these controversial materials in a more positive way?
3. What role can the media play in reporting incidents of this type?
4. What effect does an incident of this type have on the credibility of the school board?

C. Seditious Aspects

Books presenting unpopular political views may come under close scrutiny. Writings which do not support the status quo and particularly books which present a viewpoint seen as "socialist" or "communist" may be perceived as being "seditious" and attempts at censorship may be made upon them. One writer believes that some books, such as *Catcher in the Rye,* are targets of critics, not because of references to sex, but because they are thought to teach disrespect for the adult establishment (72). Censorship of material that does not support the existing system, by omission of significant information or through inadequate treatment, is subtle but common. Atnikov,

Oleson and McRuer (137), in their study of Manitoba social studies textbooks, claim that alien political systems receive very biased treatment. The use of negative evaluative terms, lack of objectivity and omission of significant information are often unjustified.

Some teachers, faced with the dilemma of using biased materials, may opt for an approach that helps students become aware of the bias. One teacher and her husband complained to the British Columbia Department of Education about a Grade 6 social studies text, *Let's Visit Russia,* published by Longmans Canada. The book, approved by the department, contains the following statements: the U.S.S.R. is solely responsible for wars in Vietnam, Korea, and the Middle East; the United States saved all of Europe, including Greece and Turkey, from becoming Communist; Russians and Americans have been at war since 1945; and Russians rarely keep promises. The North Vancouver school board pointed out the book's "objectionable passages" to the department of education and instructed teachers to use the offensive passages "for instructional purposes, though not as intended by the authors," to develop critical thinking among students (25). The next day the department withdrew the book from classroom use. It appeared that the textbook selection committee had ordered a British version, which does not contain the same conclusions, but Longmans had sent the American edition (95).

A recent dilemma of a different sort occurred in Manitoba over a textbook developed by a special department of the (then NDP) government. The textbook was entitled *Co-operative Outlooks* and cost over one million dollars to develop. The book focuses on the development of co-operatives as business ventures. The government changed just before the books were to be distributed, and somehow they never found their way into schools, although teachers were free to use them if they wished. Conservative Economic Development Minister Frank Johnson claimed that the illustrations always "show the bad guys as the free enterprisers." One Conservative backbencher said he would not want his children or his grandchildren exposed to such books at a young age. Another Conservative member called the books "socialist junk." The books were eventually sold at a discount price to an institution in Saskatchewan, a province with an NDP government (107).

Any book that suggests a communist philosophy may be challenged. In Toronto, a parent objected to the presence of an issue of the magazine *Peking Review,* on the grounds that it would "make students susceptible to communist propaganda" (142, p. 54). Figure 3 outlines a complaint concerning the children's book *Mao-Tse-Tung.* This short book was moved to a part of the library accessible only to teachers (14).

Figure 3:

BOOK BAN REQUEST TO BE INVESTIGATED

By Tim Haverluck

A request by a parent of a Fort Garry elementary student to "withdraw from all students in the division" a small book with the title Mao Tse Tung was shunted to an investigative committee Monday night by the Fort Garry school board.

The tiny volume, in the shape of most children's fairytale books and written in much the same style, describes the life of Mao Tse Tung, founder of modern Red China.

The offended parent, whose name wasn't revealed, said the book "perpetuates in young minds communist doctrine which rejects the Judeo-Christian concept of God." The concerned parent also claimed the book, of which only a single copy exists in the entire school division library system, and isn't required reading by any student, taught "value judgements" such as "rich is evil" and "Mao was the people's liberator."

From "Book Ban Request To Be Investigated" by Tim Haverluck, WINNIPEG FREE PRESS, June 1, 1978, p.42, reprinted by permission of the WINNIPEG FREE PRESS.

Figure 3: Something to think about

1. Should the study of other political systems be a part of the curriculum in Canadian schools? At what level could such studies best be taught?
2. With which political systems are Canadian children most familiar: Canadian, American, European, Russian or Chinese? Why? With which political systems should they be familiar? Why? An exploration of this topic with children might prove interesting.
3. How valid is the statement that teaching about alternative political philosophies "perpetuates in young minds communist doctrine"?
4. Does a parent have the right to demand that a book be withdrawn from all students?
5. Should materials that examine the Canadian economic and political system be a part of a child's education? Should children learn to question the status quo?
6. Is censorship of materials that present an alien political system in

an unbiased or even favourably biased manner justified? Should unfavourably biased materials be censored? If so, why?

D. Heretical Aspects

Material which is heretical in the Judeo-Christian context may be objected to. Frequently groups accusing the school of being opposed to "Judeo-Christian values" do not attack specific books but rather make general accusations about the whole school system. However, specific books are also identified, and the objections raised are often closely linked with immorality, communism, and the use of profanity, illustrated by the references to Christian values in Figures 2, 3 and 4. Many of the people who express concerns in this area are sincerely and genuinely interested in training and educating their children in what they consider to be the best way. Figure 4 illustrates the deep religious feelings of one parent concerning the deepening rift in Virden, Manitoba, over the issue of censorship and its impact on the children of the community.

In Peterborough, Ontario, *Flowers for Algernon* was banned from school following various complaints, including the accusation that it was atheistic (138, pp. 146-7).

In Huron County, Ontario, the Board of Education removed *The Diviners* as an approved book for senior high school English courses. They did not succeed, however, in having *Of Mice and Men* and *Catcher in the Rye* banned. Attempts to ban books in Huron County failed in 1977, but in 1978, in response to numerous group complaints, *The Diviners* was removed from the reading list for schools in that area. A leader of one of the pro-banning groups said of the book *Of Mice and Men,* "I counted 40 examples in the first 40 pages of straight spitting in the face of God." (6, 29, 108).

Figure 4:

Censorship not the issue in textbook controversy

by VERNA DUFFIELD

I feel very concerned about the controversy in the Virden area about books being used in our high school. It started with concerned parents feeling their children were being taught from books which contained things they did not approve of. There was no thought of book burning, witch hunting or accusing teachers of teaching pornography.

The parents who started it love

Jesus deeply. To have His name used as a swear word in the books their children are using is a terrible thing, just as it would be to anyone to hear the name of someone they love used as a swear word. We believe Heaven and Hell are real places. To see them used as slang or swear words in school books is of real concern to us. There may be parents to whom this is of no concern so they, I am sure, would find it difficult to understand why we would take such a stand. I don't believe most parents who swear like to hear their children swear. Most would not deliberately teach their children to swear.

I wonder if the teachers using these books really realize the shock some of them cause some parents. I wonder if they have been teaching them so long that any shock impact would have ceased to be there. What we are asking is, "Are there no books available to teach the lessons that teachers and parents wish taught which do not contain filthy words, the use of the Lord's name and others, such as Hell, as swear words or any reference to sex in an obscene manner?"

We are not prudes or ostriches. We do know sex exists. But it was certainly not meant to be the sick perversion it is today in our permissive society. Can we not have our young people taught that life could and should be better? They are just beginning their adult lives. Is it stupid to want them to be taught in school how to live in the best way possible?

... I am concerned that the ministers of our town have taken opposite stands. Don't we all love our children and want what's best for them? Can this problem not be worked out with co-operation and in concern for our children, not in anger and hostility.

Before the open meeting tonight please let's all think rationally and with real concern for our children and teachers. It is only natural for the teachers to defend themselves and the books they are using. We all do that when we feel we are being attacked. Deep down in their hearts surely they must be thinking about the books they are using and wondering what is right and wrong in them.

Can we not use this controversy as a stepping stone to a better education and life for our young people? Let's forget about such nonsense as book burning and witch hunting and try to do what's best for everyone and consider everyone's feeling, not just our own. If this meeting continues in the same way as things have so far we may as well forget about the books. We will have taught our young people by example something I don't believe we want them to learn.

I beg of you, forget about censorship. It should not even be considered here. These are not adults we are dealing with who can choose for themselves what they read. These are young teen-agers who are not yet capable of knowing what is best. They are not choosing these books. The choice is made by adults. So we already have censorship. Only concern for our young people and how to help them live their lives in a meaningful way should be important. What the teacher reads at home is none of my business and if I tried to tell him what he could or couldn't read, that would be censorship. I definitely feel it is my business what he gives my child to read.

Let us attend this meeting with respect and concern for each other and our young people. I don't know if representatives of the newspapers and television will be at the meeting or not. If they are I hope we will all act like intelligent, mature people. If we lose our tempers and say angry things to each other, we will only prove to the world and our teen-agers that we are not really concerned about the real issue at all. We are just interested in proving we are right and someone else is wrong and that the real concern all parents have for their children comes second.

I don't really care if I am right or wrong. I just want to have the best books available taught in our high schools.

From "Censorship not the issue in textbook controversy"
by Verna Duffield, BRANDON SUN, Nov. 30, 1978, p.4,
reprinted by permission of Verna Duffield and the BRANDON SUN.

Figure 4: Something to think about

1. In this community, the school system was accused of being "narrow-minded in its viewpoint" and unwilling to "respond to any other views ... but one-track secularism" (49). How legitimate is this complaint? Is the point of view desired by the parents in this community ever presented in schools? Should it be? Why or why not?
2. How should a superintendent handle a tense situation such as this?
3. At one point in this incident, some individuals refused to meet with those holding opposing views. Is there a point at which a refusal to engage in dialogue is beneficial in solving the dilemma?
4. Should the librarian have removed the books before the uproar developed?
5. Duffield makes the statement: "I definitely feel it is my business what he (the teacher) gives my child to read." Whose business is it to educate children? Sometimes parents request that their children study materials other than the ones assigned by the teacher. Will this create undue peer pressure on children? Would the child receive adequate instruction on the alternative book? How can home and school work together in educating children?
6. How should concerned parents deal with materials presenting beliefs other than their own?
7. How involved should teachers be in presenting moral issues? Should they avoid discussions on ethics? Can they?
8. What is the place of school books presenting the "wrong" viewpoint in a relatively homogeneous community?

E. Violent Aspects

Objections to violence on television and movie screens have increased in recent years, and a heightened sensitivity to forms of violence may be permeating certain groups. The arguments over the effects of exposure to violence range from one end of the spectrum to the other. On the one hand, violence can act as catharsis in young minds and make it possible for children to deal with the natural human urges that are violent. A more modern position, on the other hand, is that increased exposure to violence in magazines and on television fosters violent behaviour in young people. While no concrete proof for the latter argument has emerged, the increasing amount of violence present in our society remains a serious problem.

In Victoria, B.C., the Ministry of Education withdrew the book *Incentives* from the Grade 8 curriculum and the book *Strawberries and Other Secrets* from the Grade 9 curriculum after both adults and students complained about the episodes of violence and the racial and sexual stereotyping in the books. In British Columbia, 85,000 copies were withdrawn, representing a total expenditure of $127,000 (113, see also figure 8).

An unpublished survey of Manitoba high school students revealed rather blasé attitudes towards violence in literature (145). The researcher attributed this lack of concern or reaction to the glut of violence and sensationalism on television and movie screens. Yet, according to the same survey, sex and obscenity stir up considerable agitation in students. The implications of these findings would be interesting to explore. It may be difficult to judge the point at which parents, if not students, will become upset by violence in literature, as indicated by the following incidents.

In St. Boniface, Manitoba, a parent complained about the picture book *Bang, Bang, You're Dead.* No one wins in this story about two groups of children who decide to have a war game, arm themselves with sticks, rocks and baseball bats and proceed to battle each other. The moral is that violence is no way to solve a problem (106). Even though the viewpoint is obviously anti-violent, the book is not acceptable to some parents.

In St. Catherines, Ontario (96), a psychologist strongly objected to a story in a Grade 2 reader as being "violent, sadistic and savage." The story is about what happens to little boys who are bold enough to wander around the corner: they are stuffed into a sack by a man who takes them home to dismember and eat them. The publisher of the book admitted that he was at fault for not using illustrations to show that the story is indeed a fairy tale. The story was dropped from the Grade 2 reading program.

On the other hand, the violence contained in fairy tales has been defended as a way of dealing with strong human instinct. Diluting the violence in fairy or other moral tales may be a means of censoring their impact. A professor of children's literature says that, over the years, many fairy tales have been censored. For example, in the 1657 version of *Little Red Riding Hood*, the wolf eats the grandmother and later talks the pretty heroine into undressing and getting into bed with him, at which point he eats her up. In the Grimm's version of 1812, the little girl is eaten but is rescued when a woodcutter cuts open the wolf. The professor notes that all references to warning, eating or death have been censored out of all versions of this tale published since 1972. He states, "The old version flirts with things that disturb you as any good literature does. I think the children getting the new [versions] are the ones who are not going to be interested in reading." (97)

Figure 5, a, b and c, includes an excerpt from a fairy tale, a letter of objection from a parent, and the school librarian's response.

Figure 5a:

"Now, I'm coming to gobble you up!" roared the troll.
"Well, come along! I've got two spears,
And I'll poke your eyeballs out at your ears.
I've got besides two great big stones,
And I'll crush you to bits, body and bones."

Asbjornsen, P.C. and J.E. Moe. THE THREE BILLY GOATS GRUFF.
Harcourt, Brace & World, 1957. From THE THREE BILLY GOATS GRUFF,
illustrated and © 1957 by Marcia Brown.
Reproduced by permission of Harcourt Brace Jovanovich, Inc.

Figure 5b: A letter of complaint to a school

Dear Library Teacher,

I really object to the way this book is written. I don't feel that kids in Grades 1 and 2 need to read things like "I'll poke your eyeballs out at your ears." What happened to the old version of the book? Unfortunately both my children have brought this awful book home which I refused to let them read. This has been the only book I've objected to. I just don't think it's suitable for primary children.

Reprinted by permission of L. Fitzsimmons.

Figure 5c: Letter of response from a school librarian

February 2, 1978.

Dear Mrs. —————,

Thank-you for your letter of concern regarding the book *The Three Billy Goats Gruff* which both Matthew and Jennifer brought home.

I sympathize with your concern over the violence in the book, but I hope you will allow me to explain why such a book appears in school libraries.

As you are probably aware, belief in fairies began back in the Middle Ages where they became known as the "good" noble fairies or the "evil" household fairies. The latter became more commonly known as elves, goblins, kobolds, leprechauns, or trolls. Over the years tales concerning them were embellished by the story-tellers to demonstrate some moral. In *The Three Billy Goat's Gruff* the theme was punishment for selfishness, in *Little Red Riding Hood* the wolf is punished as the child learns not to speak to strangers, and in *Hansel and Gretel* the witch is burned in her own oven for luring the children away from their home.

Encyclopedia International Volume 7, page 223 describes their appeal for children, "folk tales are enjoyed by children because of their dramatic qualities and strong plots; they are important in developing imagination."

Most fairy tales do contain strong violence to demonstrate the difference between good and evil.

I do not hope to change your point of view and I welcome your comments on any library material. I do wish to explain though that there is a place in a child's world for a fairy tale, just as there has been for hundreds of years.

I am enclosing another version of the tale which you might like to read to your children. Thank-you once again for your concern.

Sincerely, _____

Reprinted by permission of L. Fitzsimmons.

Figures 5a, 5b, 5c: Something to think about

1. How should violence be defined?
2. Is there any reason why materials that contain violence might be taught in schools? Is the age of students a factor in making this decision?
3. How might reading violent episodes contained in fairy tales affect young children?
4. Can the difference between good and evil be illustrated dramatically without using violence? Is the force of evil weakened if the violence is weakened? Will "revised" stories have the same intrinsic appeal that the original stories have?
5. Should students be protected from the knowledge of the continuing violence in the world today?
6. Does the moral context in which a violent episode is presented have a bearing on the decision whether or not books foster violence?

F. Racist Aspects

The Report of the Task Force on Text Book Evaluation (153) to the Manitoba Minister of Education showed that poor representation or under-representation of "ethnicity, visible minorities, women, immigrants, status, social class" are the most frequently mentioned complaints made about textbooks. It also related these criticisms to "errors of omission, errors of commission, imbalanced presentations, stereotyped illustrations, and avoidance of human rights issues." When textbooks that are faulty in this manner are used with nothing to conteract the bias, one might say that opposing or unpopular or unusual viewpoints, or even factual and realistic information, have been "censored." At the same time, the question of censorship is brought to the fore when attempts are made to remove material because of bias.

Various groups have put forward complaints centring on unfavourable bias toward themselves or others in school books. The treatment of Canada's native people in school texts has often been criticized. In 1969, the Manitoba Human Rights Commission criticized school history texts for "attitudes of contempt toward ancient Indian religious beliefs and customs" (2). An evaluation by the Manitoba Indian Brotherhood of social studies textbooks in elementary schools states that these textbooks "give a derogatory and incomplete picture of the Canadian Indian" (158).

The Greater Victoria school board was divided over the continued use of a story about Almighty Voice in *Under Canadian Skies*, a Grade 5 reader. School trustee Walter Donald urged the Department of Education to withdraw the book because the story suggests that the violence used against Almighty Voice was justified. Another trustee opposed the story on the grounds that it stereotypes native peoples by using phrases like "heap big indian" and "squaws" (61).

The British Columbia Association of Non-Status Indians urged removal of the story "The Long Arm of the Law" from the curriculum. Brian Maracle, educational director for the association, commented, "Who knows how many thousands of kids' minds have been poisoned by this type of thing? Our men are not bucks and braves and our women are not squaws. We do not say 'heap big Indian' and things like that" (62).

In 1971 Atnikov et al. (137) criticized Manitoba social studies textbooks for prejudicial treatment of blacks and slavery, glorification of Christians, stereotyping of Indians, and inadequate portrayals of the contemporary status of Indians, French Canadians and immigrant groups. The six texts which they considered to be the worst offenders have since been removed from the approved list of social studies textbooks in Manitoba.

While the social studies texts taught in Canadian schools should not belittle important sectors of the population, censoring certain passages that present difficulties will not always solve the problem. A positive and more historically accurate picture of these peoples' achievements is what is needed to counteract prejudice.

Keith Wilson, a writer of social studies books intended for classroom use, remarked that non-fiction books are scrutinized in an ahistorical manner by curriculum committees of provincial departments of education. He states:

> While obviously you don't want to include anything that unnecessarily denigrates a group, you should be able to use quotes that in the context of the time, let's say a hundred years ago, illustrate what somebody else thought. The trouble is that the words are often taken as your opinion of that group today, and so you play it safe

and omit. People should be judged in the moral context of the time, not today's. "If you can't say something good, don't say it" becomes the operating rule. This is one form of censorship. In fact, it's censorship by omission. You become cautious and that leads to a tendency, if you don't watch it, of everything becoming a bland sameness which, of course, defeats your very object in the first place (127).

* For the reader's information, the guidelines to minimize prejudice and bias in textbooks have been reproduced in Appendix III.

An example of censoring an appreciation of history might be a case in which Jacques Cartier's journals are edited to delete his reference to the native population as "savages." Certainly, there should be some distinction between portraying a historical imperialist attitude and maintaining that attitude today, a distinction that can be taught by including counter-balancing books on the course of study.

Bias towards Indians is only one bias that has been noted in school books. A Toronto Board of Education subcommittee on race relations was told that the *Merchant of Venice* and *Huckleberry Finn* should be removed from the curriculum because they promote racism (138, p. 56). In this case the bias was against Jews and Blacks respectively. In Winnipeg, following a complaint from a school trustee, the study of *Huckleberry Finn* was made optional on the Grade 11 Gordon Bell High School reading list. Although the novel was approved by the Curriculum Branch of the Manitoba Department of Education, it was objected to because of its apparently racist nature (145, p. 1).

Other instances of complaints on the grounds of racism are not hard to come by. As mentioned earlier, the books *Incentives* and *Strawberries and Other Secrets* were removed from B.C. schools, in part because they contain racial prejudice (113). In Toronto, Ontario, in the Borough of North York, schools removed the dust covers from George Orwell's *Animal Farm* after complaints of anti-Semitism were lodged. The cover in question depicts two pigs, one of them with "what could be interpreted as a Star of David around its neck" (109). A Jewish parent became upset on reading a two-page biography of St. Paul from a twenty-volume set of books, *Great Leaders,* because it "blames the Jews for killing Christ" (69).

German-born Canadians presented a brief to the Metropolitan Toronto study group on racism, citing unfair treatment of Germans in school textbooks. They suggested that "all reading matter, especially comics and children's pre-school and school books, be removed from circulation, which contain excessive stereotyping and slander." The brief attacked comic book covers detailing sadism and sex crimes involving persons dressed in Nazi uniforms (18).

Two texts containing information on the Middle East political situation were dropped in Ontario due to pressure from Moslem minority groups (66). A response to this move is given in Figure 6. The response raises some interesting questions as to whether it is possible to write material without involving bias of some sort.

Figure 6:

Censoring history texts supine surrender: historian

Thought control exercised by the state is rightly feared by anyone living in a "free" society. Yet, while we express our horror when confronted by each fresh piece of evidence from within the various totalitarian systems of our age, we seem amazingly apathetic in the face of evidence of thought control within our own society.

Possibly this is because our measures of thought control usually masquerade as a response to pressure group activism: and such activism, of course, is always praiseworthy in a democracy. However, pressure groups can be very dangerous, especially when they subserve the interests of racial-nationalism. Even more so when they frighten our governments into collusion with their purposes.

It seems to me that the Ontario Department of Education is guilty of just such collusion. Pressured by a Moslem-Canadian group it has ordered the removal of a number of textbooks from its list of books approved for use in Ontario Schools (Circular 14). Paul Fleck, the director of the department's Curriculum Development Branch, has explained that the censorship has been imposed as a result of submissions made by Professors L.M. Kenny and J.R. Blackburn of the University of Toronto's Islamic Studies department, and by the Canadian Society of Moslems. The three reports submitted to the department by these people level charges of bias and inaccuracy against a considerable number of books listed in Circular 14 and the department has obligingly removed many of the guilty books from its approved list. Concerning five of the censored books Mr. Fleck remarks that his ban may be lifted if "the publishers of these books will find it possible to revise the books in a manner to meet the concerns which have been expressed." That is, our Government will approve textbooks only if they are agreeable to the sentiments of Canadian Moslems.

I have read the reports on which Mr. Fleck says he based his decision and I have examined carefully several of the books which have been removed from the list. I have also written or co-authored two books which are still (by the grace of God and the department) on the approved list. On the basis of this experience I charge the department with supine surrender to a special interest group and a wilful disregard of the fundamentals of liberal education.

The principal charges against the books which have been proscribed is that they show "Western" bias, contain some inaccuracies and do not always bring their accounts of Middle Eastern affairs down to the present day. The Kenny-Blackburn submission says "very seldom do the authors seem able to view Middle Eastern history from the inside; rather the viewpoint generally remains parochial and Western-oriented." The implication is that "Western" scholars are by definition parochial and that the Middle East can only be written about by people who live there or have come from there. This is nonsense. One might ask these successful censors who writes Moslem textbooks and whether these books seek Jewish authors for their passages on Palestine and Israel. The books I examined are not perfect but not one of them merits censorship on the grounds taken by Moslem critics.

On the question of biased selection of facts no one who has ever attempted to compress any history into a textbook will accept the implicit demand for "objectivity" and "comprehensiveness" on all aspects of the subject. I'm sure that American-Canadians could become just as angry with my account of American history as Moslems become when faced with "Western" accounts of Ottoman and Middle Eastern history. The answer to the problem is not to censor existing "approved texts" but to write new ones. Perhaps Professors Kenny and Blackburn will oblige us. I would look forward with extreme interest to reading their non-parochial, non-Western-oriented account of Israel in the context of modern world history.

The very essence of liberal education is variety and comparison of opinion. Total objectivity in a necessarily compressed textbook is, by any definition, impossible. While we may or may not agree with the concept of an approved list of such books, at least we may expect that the books selected will not be officially tampered with, that we can respect the integrity of the scholars who write them, and that we will keep open the door to competitive interpretations.

To remove a book because interested critics say that its "treatment of the Middle East and its peoples in recent times is not altogether free of bias, both in language and by omission of related facts" is an admission of abject denial of independence. Not just the director of the Curriculum Development Branch, but the Minister himself should be held directly culpable.

Kenneth McNaught
Department of History
University of Toronto

From "Censoring history texts supine surrender: historian"
by Kenneth McNaught, GLOBE AND MAIL, Oct. 30, 1976, p.7,
reprinted by permission of Kenneth McNaught and THE GLOBE AND MAIL,
Toronto.

Figure 6: Something to think about

1. Is it possible to write an unbiased textbook? Is there a measurable difference between bias and inaccuracy?
2. Should books be removed when they contain racial stereotyping or bias against any minority group? Should they be used if nothing better is available?
3. In this case, did the Department of Education act as a censor?
4. Consider Professor McNaught's statement that he wishes to "keep open the door to competitive interpretations" in light of other school books available on Middle Eastern affairs. Is any interpretation acceptable, as long as it is one of several? Should one interpretation be favoured over another? If so, on what basis?

G. Sexist Aspects

Improving the Image of Women in Textbooks gives the following definition of sexist textbooks:

> Textbooks are sexist if they omit the actions and achievements of women, if they demean women by using patronizing language, or if they show women or men only in stereotyped roles with less than the full range of human interests, traits, and capabilities. The actual role of sexism in society, past and present, should not be ignored: and, where appropriate, textbooks can discuss sexism as an important phenomenon without reflecting or reinforcing sexist bias (144).

One study written by Women for Non-Sexist Education (161) claims that sexism still exists in books used at the primary level. The authors observe that females are usually presented in passive roles while males are shown to be active participants. Careers are defined by sex, illustrations centre on male characters. In this study, specific examples are given and individual language arts textbooks are analysed. One might argue that the personhood of women has been censored by omission in these biased texts. Although the study recommends that biased textbooks be withdrawn from use, the authors recognize that the school system cannot change overnight. They recommend ways in which teachers can confront the stereotypes they find in school books and ways they can help children understand and overcome the implications of bias.

The title page for a study on the same subject by the Ad Hoc Committee Respecting the Status of Women in the North York System is given in Figure 7. In the study, many primary textbooks are severely criticized for promoting sexism. Example after example is given.

Figure 7:

EXCERPT FROM:

INTERIM REPORT NO. 2
AD HOC COMMITTEE RESPECTING THE STATUS OF WOMEN
IN THE NORTH YORK SYSTEM

3 June 1975

To the Chairman and Members of the
Management and Academic Program Committee

THIS REPORT WAS FORWARDED TO, BUT NOT CONSIDERED BY, THE MANAGEMENT AND ACADEMIC PROGRAM COMMITTEE, NORTH YORK BOARD OF EDUCATION on 3 JUNE 1975

"8. Print Media

The report on print media, based on a survey of the most frequently used grades 1, 2 and 3 readers in the Borough of North York, is submitted in accordance with the following terms of reference of the Ad Hoc Committee respecting the Status of Women: (i) the identification and elimination of all teaching materials which perpetuate a bias based on sex; (ii) the implementation of courses designed specifically to stress the role of women in our past and current society; and (iii) the provision of professional development for all staff to assist them in the role of change agents relating to the elimination of sex stereotyped roles in society.

THE RAPE OF CHILDREN'S MINDS

From "Interim Report No. 2, Ad Hoc Committee Respecting the Status of Women in the North York System" reproduced by permission of The Board of Education for the City of North York.

A study for the Nova Scotia Human Rights Commission (141) gives numerous examples of sexism in textbooks used in Canadian schools. The Commission's guidelines for eliminating sexism in primary language arts textbooks can be found in Appendix IV. As with the guidelines for removing racial bias in Appendix III, the tension between intellectual freedom and removing bias becomes apparent.

The removal of biased textbooks often conflicts with budget restrictions imposed on departments of education. In one instance, the British Columbia Minister of Education responded to criticism by saying that sexist textbooks could not be removed immediately; however, when the old textbooks needed replacing (i.e. when they had worn out), every effort would be made to find better ones (9). A special consultant was appointed to advise on sexual stereotyping in textbooks and curriculum (104).

Figure 8 outlines the details of a controversy in British Columbia over the book *Strawberries and Other Secrets,* which was accused of being sexist.

In spite of these incidents, Fasick and England in their study (122) found that sexism in library books was not considered to be as objectionable as racism.

Figure 7: Something to think about

1. Can all teaching materials that perpetuate a sexist attitude be removed from schools? What would this step involve?
2. How should one respond to persons who feel that male/female roles need to be defined traditionally?
3. Does the portrayal of boys as active participants and of girls as passive observers have an effect on children's self-perceptions?
4. Is there a method by which a teacher or parent can lessen the effect of sexism in otherwise valuable books?
5. Is there a difference between censorship and using the guidelines to eliminate sexism contained in Appendix V?
6. How significant is it that the school board did not consider the report submitted by the North York Ad Hoc Committee?

Figure 8: Something to think about

1. Although the Status of Women Committee felt that *Strawberries and Other Secrets* was not suitable for schools, they did not feel the

book was withdrawn in an appropriate manner. How might the situation have been handled more positively?

2. Once criticism of a book is widely known, should teachers continue to use it as a supplementary teaching resource in order to teach particular themes, styles, characterizations, etc.? How many teachers would be aware of the criticisms?

3. Should offensive material be removed upon receipt of a complaint? after reconsideration? when there is something to replace the material? Who should be involved in reconsideration procedures?

Figure 8:

A Mysterious Case of Forbidden Fruit

Atlin Elementary & Junior
Sec. School
P.O. Box 83, Atlin, B.C.
V0W 1A0

October 19, 1978

Ms. Berenice Wood
6626 Kingsway
Burnaby, B.C.
V5E 1H1

Dear Ms. Wood:

Re: school department circular No. 68 item C "Titles Deleted and No Longer Authorized for Use by the Ministry."

I wish to know the rationale given by the Ministry for its removal of *Incentives* and *Strawberries and Other Secrets* from the prescribed textbook list. Thank you.

Yours truly,

Mary-Dawn Rippell

The B.C.E.T.A. has received a number of other letters and calls, concerning the reason for the deletion of *Strawberries and Other Secrets* from the authorized list of books and voicing objections to the book's deletion. Preparing a satisfactory answer for Ms. Rippell and others has been far from simple, but in brief the following information has come to light.

From the Ministry of Education came the verbal explanation that *Strawberries and Other Secrets* is objectionable for two reasons, violence and sexism (the collection of stories allegedly has only one female protagonist); therefore as an A-issue text provided to every Grade Nine student, the book is deemed to be not acceptable. As a result of the book's deletion, the copies of the text in use in Delta were apparently collected for disposal. In reaction, a group of Delta teachers sent a letter to the Ministry querying the reasons for the book's deletion but has not received an answer at presstime.

The following memorandum outlines the general situation as communicated to Mike Zlotnik of the B.C.T.F. by B.C.E.T.A. President David Bristow:

MEMORANDUM

TO: Pat Brady, Al Blakey, Bob Buzza, Jim Bowman

CC: Dave Bristow, John Church, Debby Stagg, Dulce Oikawa

FROM: Mike Zlotnik

RE: *Strawberries and Other Secrets*

November 8, 1978

On November 7, Dave Bristow, President of the B.C. English Teachers' PSA called regarding the Grade 9 English text *Strawberries and Other Secrets*. Some of the facts are not entirely clear yet but the general situation follows.

1. *Strawberries and Other Secrets* was a Grade 9 A issue short story text.

2. In June (or September?) *Strawberries . . .* was dropped from list.

3. Dave Bristow talked with Ian Parker of the Ministry. Parker indicated removal was a result of pressure from groups on the grounds that *Strawberries* . . .

   (a) had violence
   (b) had only one female protagonist.

4. Delta Superintendent is believed to have ordered books boxed.

5. Bristow has received phone calls from concerned teachers in the interior and from Delta.

6. The effect of de-listing is that *Strawberries and Other Secrets* is no longer a textbook and cannot be ordered from the Ministry. Depending on the interpretation of the circular it may or may not be used.

7. Teachers are concerned because:

   (a) They were not informed of reasons.
   (b) Many of the stories are in other anthologies.
   (c) Withdrawal leaves a void in terms of covering Core curriculum.
   (d) Consider *Strawberries* . . . to be excellent.

A telephone call to Status of Women chairperson Lynda Coplin to discuss the matter elicited the following response for *Update*. According to Lynda Coplin, the Status of Women Committee had no advance warnings that the book was being removed. She voiced her concerns on behalf of the Status of Women programme, not that the committee supports the particular book in question, but rather that its policy is to advocate the replacement of any deleted materials with revised non-sexist materials.

Copies of the following memorandum were forwarded to *Update* by both BCTF President Pat Brady and Heather Knapp, Status of Women Committee:

MEMORANDUM
(PD78 - 1509a,
November 29, 1978)

TO: Mike Zlotnik

CC: Pat Brady, Al Blakey, Bob Buzza, Jim Bowman, Dave Bristow, John Church, Debby Stagg, Dulce Oikawa, Status of Women Committee

FROM: Pearl Roberts

DATE: November 29, 1978

RE: *Strawberries and Other Secrets*

In reading the minutes of a PD Concerns meeting, I became aware that action had been taken by the BCTF regarding the removal of the Grade 9 English text, *Strawberries and Other Secrets*. The Status of Women Committee and I have also received queries about the removal of this book, which we were unable to answer because of lack of information.

The matter was discussed at the November 17/18 Status of Women Committee meeting with Ethne Erskine, curriculum consultant. Ms. Erskine referred us to Ian Parker.

What concerns me is that the Status of Women Committee did not receive copies of the memos on this topic, although it was clear from the beginning that one complaint about the textbook was its sexist bias. My other concern is that your memo of November 8 states that teachers "consider *Strawberries* . . . to be excellent." The Status of Women Committee certainly does not concur with this. *Strawberries* has been used in Status of Women workshops for years as an example of a blatantly sexist textbook. Although it may have literary merit, the text does not reflect the kinds of values that the BCTF supports.

The committee agrees that the Ministry handled the removal of the book poorly. They are looking forward to a high-quality, non-sexist replacement.

PD78-1509a
November 29, 1978
PR/jh

In discussing the issue of the book's deletion, Pat Brady stated that the B.C.T.F. will draw the attention of the Ministry to the matter at the next Deputy Minister Advisory Committee meeting. A major concern is with the process by which books are deleted and with the basis used to determine whether a specific book should be deleted.

English teachers whose classroom work is directly affected by the removal of *Strawberries and Other Secrets* — as well as other teachers who realize the effects of similar deletions on other subjects and programmes — have voiced a common concern, namely that if a book is deleted, the failure to provide a replacement text leaves a gap in the course which is ultimately detrimental to the students' education. Presumably such a text has been intended to cover an area of core curriculum. What happens, however, to the students' knowledge of core content if texts are deleted and not replaced with satisfactory alternates?

As more information concerning the particular case of *Strawberries and Other Secrets* becomes available, it will be printed in *Update*. Please address any further queries to David, B.C.E.T.A. President, or Berenice Wood, *Update* editor.

From "A Mysterious Case of Forbidden Fruit" by Berenice Wood,
UPDATE, Dec. 1978, p.6-7, reproduced by permission of Berenice Wood.

H. Labour-Related Aspects

Atnikov et al. (137) examine the inadequate representation in Canadian school books of trade unions and the labour movement. Their observations point to censorship by omission. Another study, examining the image of the Canadian labourer in the principal history textbooks used in Canada, states that working class or labour history is conspicuous by its absence from school texts. In Osborne's examination of textbooks used across Canada between 1886 and 1979, he reveals that, while modern textbooks contain more social history and moralize less overtly, social conflict is consistently minimized. Topics such as the 1837 revolts, the Riel Rebellion, and the 1919 Winnipeg Strike are mentioned, but Canada's record of working-class militance and industrial conflict is almost totally ignored. He states that...

> the school system is an area where different groups with different objectives compete: for the working class it is a potential vehicle for economic and political emancipation; for those in power, it is a vehicle of social control. To date, the Canadian working class has not been able to give much attention to its relationship with the schools, but the potential is there. And one place to begin is with the textbooks (150).

I. Nationally Sensitive Issues

According to Atnikov et al. (137), the relationship between English and French Canada is a nationally sensitive issue that is censored by omission from school curricula. Considering it was not mentioned or discussed at all in all but one of the textbooks they examined, it is not surprising that there is a "lack of understanding" between French and English Canada! Their study is supported by Paul Robinson's findings in his examination of textbooks used in the Atlantic region, which would seem to be a natural place for some understanding of the Acadians to be taught. In Ontario, a publisher was required to drop from a Grade 7 anthology a story dealing with the French-English issue before the anthology could be approved for use (138, p. 54).

In 1976, Pierre Vallières' *White Niggers of America,* which presented an understanding of Quebec separatism from the inside, was stricken from the approved list of textbooks by the Review Committee of the Peterborough County Board of Education (112).

In 1978, a Canadian government Order-in-Council prohibited the distribution of information about an international uranium cartel without the permission of the Ministry of Energy, Mines and Resources. Although the information was readily available in the U.S. *Congressional Reports,* according to Michael Dagg's article in *Feliciter,* any teacher or librarian in Canada who wanted to distribute this information for "current events" discussions would face five years in prison or a $10,000 fine or both (31).

Such incidents are rare. Nationally sensitive issues rarely make it into our school systems, since many of our textbooks are developed in the U.S. and contain only nominal Canadian references.

Opinion

The preceding pages have discussed the variety of aspects of school books that have come to the fore most frequently in textbook controversies. While some of the complaints seem rational and specific and others appear irrational and vague, it should be remembered that most complaints reflect deep-rooted opinions, feelings or ideas on the purpose of education and the values it should promote. Some people argue for a realistic presentation of the world; others for the protection of innocence. Should "good literature" be rejected because it contains isolated acts of violence, presents a sexist viewpoint or uses a swear word? Is there a difference between removing *The Merchant of Venice* or a social studies textbook when both are accused of promoting racism? What is the distinction between censorship and adhering to the guidelines in Appendices III and IV?

Thelma McCormack, in an article about feminists and censorship writes:

> The combination of the volume of pornography, the increase of sado-masochistic pornography emphasizing female abuse, and the true-to-life styles has angered many women. Feminists who in the past were unwilling to ally themselves with the cultural neanderthals trying to remove *The Diviners* from secondary school curricula are beginning to advocate censorship. In short, feminists and civil libertarians are now on a collision course (130).

McCormack is not referring directly to censorship in schools, and the type of pornography she describes probably would not be found in schools. Yet her position can be applied to the school situation.

Certain passages from certain books evoke the same anger and frustrations from some groups that the type of pornography mentioned in McCormack's statement elicits from feminists. Just as feminists respond to literature which attacks and degrades them, so anyone, whether Indian, Christian, peace-lover, capitalist, communist, or moralist, may respond to real or perceived attacks upon themselves.

Jack Kean would agree with McCormack's position, stating:
> ... Principles of intellectual freedom and the principle of promoting non-discriminatory materials for children are on a collision course. They are on this course because both positions are valuable to most of us; we find ourselves caught with internal conflicts because there is value in both positions. They are on this course because the major advocates and promoters of each fail to deal with the major positions of the other side. The advocates of intellectual freedom don't respond to those who claim that the material is biased. Those who claim material currently available is discriminatory don't seem to be at all concerned about principles of intellectual freedom. Hence the advocates of intellectual freedom find themselves using tortuous logic to support intellectual freedom. And those who are worried about discrimination seem to be ready to sacrifice all that has been gained in intellectual freedom to get rid of materials that they find inappropriate to their own beliefs (65, p. 59).

Surely when individuals opposing the current secular approach to education go to the school and find virtually no books in the school library on religion, they will feel frustrated. Maybe those persons who advocate the education of the "whole" child have forgotten about one's spiritual side. Although some novels, both on the curriculum and in the library, do address this issue, non-fiction books on religion rarely enter the school system. Have they been silently censored?

In response to an uproar in Nova Scotia over obscenity in school books, Jo Robertson writes:

> In law there is still no universal absolute definition of obscenity. It is difficult to enact legislation based on wildly differing concepts of how to control and allay psychological fear of Anglo-Saxon words, the effects of adultery and homosexuality and the very real threat of their corruptive power. The relation between books and anti-social behavior has yet to be proved beyond doubt (94).

How does one deal with these subconscious and psychological fears? How does one determine the long-range effects of reading material of various types? The point of view from which a book is written may not do anything to allay ingrained fears. *Go Ask Alice* and *Bang Bang You're Dead* were both criticized, even though they are respectively anti-drugs and anti-violence. How does one define the limits of "acceptability" in an increasingly pluralistic society? Considering the wide range of philosophies, backgrounds, lifestyles and needs of communities and students, it is doubtful if a final and unanimous conclusion can be reached as to which materials are acceptable or unacceptable in all Canadian schools.

III. Who Are the Main Characters in a School Book Controversy?

In school book controversies, the opinions of the students involved tend to be ignored. One can cite few instances where students organized and took an active part in a conflict situation. For example, when a Richmond, British Columbia, school board removed *Go Ask Alice* from the library, two thousand students objected by signing a protest petition and by registering their displeasure with the press (32). Usually, this kind of organized response does not emerge, and even if it does, one is left wondering what the effects of all the furor will be on the academic, moral or emotional growth of the child. One might suspect that students have read the material, formed negative or positive opinions and are ready to move on to new material. They might even be amused at the fervour with which adults attack or defend their school books.

Parents who are genuinely concerned about their children's education may wish to examine various educational materials. Certainly, they have the right to influence and control the education and upbringing of their own children. On the other hand, the provincial departments of education, school boards and those hired by them have been given the authority to educate the children of Canada as a whole. Problems of selection and censorship can arise when the goals and opinions of these two groups conflict. Input from government-appointed groups, such as the Human Rights Commission, and from ad hoc interest groups can add to tensions over controversial school books.

A discussion of the question "Who are the main characters in a school book controversy?" must include the following: parents and other concerned individuals outside the educational system; pressure groups; individuals within the school system such as teachers, librarians, administrators and school boards.

A. Parents and Other Individuals

Parents are often the ones to initiate complaints over what their children are reading in school, and they have the right to be heard by school personnel. The school administration can often seem unapproachable to parents, as evidenced by Robert Stamp's experiences, described in *About Schools: What Every Parent Should Know* (159). It is important that schools implement policies so that both parents and school personnel will have a chance to air their views. A single complaint from one parent should not be grounds for removal of a school book, as in the incident described in Figure 9. Nor should it ensure that the book is made unavailable to children other than the child of the parent who objects. A concerned parent might telephone or visit the school or express concern to a minister or a school board. If the school or school board has an official review procedure, the complaint can be directed in an appropriate manner.

Figure 9:

Censorship

Anne Boleyn by Evelyn Anthony has been banned from the library of a Port Credit (Ontario) high school. The book received critical praise from *The New York Times* and was recommended by the *Library Journal.* One parent objected, however, and it was removed.

From QUILL & QUIRE, April 1960, p.10.
reprinted by permission of QUILL & QUIRE

B. Pressure Groups

Looking at the more highly publicized school censorship cases, one often finds that a pressure group is involved. Recently these groups have begun to organize in a more formal way.

Renaissance International, a fundamentalist Christian organization, is active across Canada and crops up frequently in reports of school book controversies. Renaissance and groups like it are characterized by media campaigns which depend upon the sensationalism of their accusations to attract attention. The following is an excerpt from a letter to the editor written by the public relations officer of one such group:

> Why should you be forced to support the bigoted religion of materialistic humanism which can't tolerate the common sense, down-to-earth reality of eternal verities ... this well laid totalitarian plan is diabolically paving the way to socialism-communism. As it is you have no choice but to subject your children to the fanatic religion of monolithic secularism which is militant atheism. (41)

Figure 10 illustrates the use of headlines in an advertisement for a banquet sponsored by a well-known pressure group. This advertisement excited considerable controversy in the community and elicited an apology from the director of the pressure group.

Some groups issue newsletters and encourage readers to "organize coffee parties ... inform friends, relatives and neighbours ... approach church, Home and School, PTA, service clubs or other organizations" (152). One book-banning rally in Saint John, New Brunswick, invited a full choir and orchestra (84).

Pamphlets using snippets from books may be distributed at these meetings or in public places such as shopping centres and may be the only parts of the book that are read by many members of the group. One snippet collection in the Huron County controversy over *The Diviners* and other books grouped lurid quotations from the offending books with questions asked in a health class (72). June Callwood's response to this "snippet warfare" shows that extracts, like statistics, can be manipulated to suit any purpose (see Figure 11).

Some pressure groups suggest reading materials for their members. Sometimes these books contain sensational titles such as *Child Seducers, Raping of the Children,* and *Satan's Bid for Your Child.* Secular pressure groups also use sensationalism in an attempt to achieve their ends. Note the title of the brief submitted to the North York Board of Education *The Rape of Children's Minds* (see Figure 7). This brief was prepared by an *Ad Hoc* Committee respecting the Status of Women in the North York System.

In some cases, a sensational issue may be used as an election platform. As cited earlier, in October 1978, a pro-censorship candidate ran unsuccessfully for a school board seat in Virden, Manitoba. In Peterborough, Ontario, none of the school board candidates opposing the use of *The Diviners* as grade thirteen curriculum material were successful in obtaining office (see Figure 1).

Figure 10:

SEX EDUCATION K-12?!
PORNOGRAPHIC LITERATURE
PSYCHOLOGICAL TAMPERING
OF STUDENTS
INVASION OF PRIVACY?

Are you having trouble with the education your child is receiving; then don't miss the

RENAISSANCE WESTERN REGIONAL BANQUET

Guest Speaker: Dr. Robert ("Bob") Thompson

Hosted by

TERRY LEWIS
*Western Regional Director
& Family Evangelist*

SPECIAL MUSIC BY

what a beautiful day
for the lord to come again

"A successful life is one that enriches others' lives through the richness of its own." By this measure, Dr. Robert Thompson's life is a real success.

Well known and loved in many places throughout the world, Dr. Thompson has served in key leadership positions with Trinity Western College, World Vision, Mission Aviation Fellowship, Sudan Interior Mission, Gospel Recordings International, Canadian Bible Society and other organizations.

He is past Member of Parliament and National Leader of the Social Credit Party, and has served in various political delegations to the U.S.A., U.N., NATO, and overseas. His integrity and deep commitment to God and fellow man has been an inspiration to many.

Dr. Thompson's association with Trinity Western College began in 1966. He has been a member and chairman of the board of governors, professor of political science, vice president of the College, and assistant to the president. He now serves as special advisor to the president.

Dr. Thompson keeps in close contact with the world situation and travels frequently on mis-

An evangelical Christian statesman, missionary, business man, author, and educator. Editor, ENCOUNTER.

sion assignments around the world. He is a prominent speaker and consultant on business and education management and international developement.

A fitting tribute to Dr. Thompson in appreciation of his many contributions will be a major classroom facility to be built in 1980 on the TWC campus: The Robert N. Thompson Business and Communications Centre. It will also include a 150-seat lecture theatre, faculty and administrative offices, and the Institute of Aviation.

Date: FEBRUARY 22nd
Cost: $5.00 PER PERSON
Tickets Available: EVANGELICAL FREE CHURCH, STEINBACH OR PHONE 284-2219 or 1-326-6836

From THE CARILLON, Feb. 20, 1980, p.9e,
reproduced by permission of THE CARILLON and Renaissance International.

Figure 10: Something to think about

1. Does the advertisement foster good relations between home and school? Does it encourage co-operation and trust?
2. Will the advertisement prompt parents to positive, constructive action? Does it encourage a diplomatic approach?
3. What will be the effect of such meetings and publicity on the conscientious and hard-working teacher? Will it encourage greater effort, or will it simply discourage?
4. The person who is relatively uninvolved or uninformed about current educational methods receives a certain impression from this advertisement. What is it? Is it valid?
5. Behind all the sensationalism and name-calling, what might be the concerns of parents who respond to this advertisement? Are their concerns legitimate?

Figure 11:

These are the sentences taken from J.D. Salinger's *The Catcher in the Rye* circulated to parents in Huron County:

☐ Page 22: "He started cleaning his Goddam fingernails with the end of a match."

☐ Page 32: "Jane said he was supposed to be a playwright or some Goddam thing, but all I ever saw him do was booze all the time and listen to every Goddam mystery on the radio, run around the Goddam house, naked."

☐ Page 192: " 'What the hellya doing?' I said. 'Nothing, I'm simply sitting here.' 'What're ya doing anyway?' I said over again. I didn't know what the hell to say — I mean I was as embarrassed as hell. 'How bout keeping your voice down? I'm simply sitting here.' 'I have to go anyway,' I said. Boy, was I nervous. I started putting on my damn pants in the dark. I could hardly get them on I was so damn nervous."

The Writers' Union doesn't believe that those three passages give an insight into Salinger's masterpiece on the subject of adolescent agony. As last year's chairman of the Union's political committee, responsible for combating censorship, I proposed that we circulate another extract from that book, one on which the title is based and presumably Salinger's own statement of what the book is about. It is this:

☐ Page 173: "Anyway, I keep picturing all these little kids playing some game in this big field of rye and all. Thousands of little kids, and nobody's around — nobody big, I mean — except me. And I'm standing on the edge of some crazy cliff. What I have to do, I have to catch everybody if they start to go over the cliff — I mean if they're running and they don't look where they're going I have to come out from somewhere and catch them. That's all I'd do all day. I'd be the catcher in the rye and all. I know it's crazy, but that's the only thing I'd really like to be."

Marian Hebb, the Writers' Union legal consultant, demolished that suggestion. She said, in essence, one snippet is as irresponsible to a book as another. She's right.

From "Reason not Passion" by June Callwood,
BOOKS IN CANADA, Nov. 1979, p.6, reprinted by permission of June Callwood.

Figure 11: Something to think about

1. In what ways can the circulation of snippets affect attitudes toward literature? Are the above snippets a fair representation of *Catcher in the Rye?* Having read just the snippets of either the Writers' Union or the Huron County parents, can one formulate an impression of the entire book?
2. What are the effects of "snippet warfare" and book-banning campaigns on the children involved? Will their curiosity about the offending books be aroused? Are they likely to read the books with an open mind? How might the reading of snippets influence the student's reading of a particular book?
3. Is snippet circulation a positive method of letting parents know what their children are reading? Is there a better way? How?

Pressure groups may achieve their aims, as did the Moslem group which effected the removal of two texts in Ontario (see also figure 6, 66). On the other hand, they may meet substantial opposition from other factions in the community. In Virden, Manitoba, minister opposed minister and politician opposed politician over the censorship issue (35, Figure 4). This case is outlined in Chapter II.

Counteracting pressure groups may be formed, such as the Society for Freedom of Choice. This society was formed in Huron County, Ontario, in response to attempts to remove from the school curriculum such books as *Of Mice and Men, The Diviners* and *Catcher in the Rye.* The Society for Freedom of Choice is a pressure group dedicated to protecting individual rights and intellectual freedom. This group failed to have *The Diviners* reinstated on the high school reading list. Because the pro-banning pressure group had relied heavily on snippets from the offending books, the Society for Freedom of Choice made a point of requesting that board members read material in its entirety before coming to a decision (6, 29).

Petitions demanding that books be removed may be countered by petitions defending the books. A 236-signature petition requesting that *Catcher in the Rye* and *The Apprenticeship of Duddy Kravitz* be retained was presented to Ontario's York County board of education in October, 1976 (82). In this case, the anti-banning group was successful in ensuring that the books remained in the schools.

Pressure groups may submit resolutions and briefs to conferences and school boards. The Renaissance brief submitted to the St. Vital, Manitoba School Board (68) and the Parents of German Descent brief presented to the Metropolitan Toronto Study Group on Racism (18) are examples. The latter group was concerned about Nazi and German stereotyping in school books, and their actions illustrate that while many pressure groups have a religious base, there are pressure groups whose concerns are secular.

The Writers' Union of Canada has actively participated in debates on censorship. It has sponsored public forums and will provide guest speakers for meetings in order to defuse the kind of emotional pressure exerted by pro-banning groups. In 1978 Governor General's Award-winning writer Alice Munro, Writers' Union president June Callwood and children's library specialist Janet Lunn appeared at a public meeting in Huron County at the request of the high school English teacher, despite the objections of the Halton Renaissance organization. In another case, the Union found itself defending, via a written brief, the inclusion of Harlequin Romances along with *The Diviners* on a supplementary reading list for a course on women in contemporary literature (117).

In June 1978, the Book and Periodical Development Council formed the Committee for Freedom of Expression. Members included the Association of Canadian Publishers, the Canadian Book Publishers Council, Periodical Distributors of Canada, the Canadian Library Association, the Canadian Periodical Publishers Association, the Writers' Union of Canada, and the League of Canadian Poets. The Committee supports individuals involved in book-banning controversies. especially at the school board level, and presents a unified voice on other issues of censorship, such as the withholding of government grants. The committee also developed an information booklet for teachers and school trustees (163).

Pressure groups such as Renaissance work from the premise that the public school system is so unsatisfactory that it should be rejected outright. Others, such as the Women for Non-Sexist Education, base their actions on the belief that, although the existing system has flaws, it can be improved. The latter may be better acquainted with the school system; their recommendations may tend to be positive, concrete and supported by in-depth studies; and they may present research or opinions to the various bodies who have the authority to make changes in curriculum, such as school boards and departments of education. They may also make suggestions to publishers, teachers, and the general public.

Examples of reports from such groups include *Canadian Books in Canadian Schools* (162), a detailed study by the Work Group on Educational and Library Materials; *A Study of Social Studies Textbooks Approved for Use in Manitoba* (137) and *Confronting the Stereotypes: Handbook on Bias at the Primary Level* (161), both prepared for the Manitoba Human Rights Commission; *Guidelines for Eliminating Sexism in Readers* (Appendix IV) from the Nova Scotia Human Rights Commission; and "Guidelines to Minimize Prejudice and Bias" from the *Report of the Task Force on Textbook Evaluation to the Honourable Ben Hanuschak, Minister of Education, Manitoba* (Appendix III).

Pressure groups certainly have the right to form, express opinions and exert pressure on the school system. Yet teachers, administrators, parents and others should be aware of the motivations and tactics of any specific group before supporting it or yielding to it. Unless school boards develop procedures for dealing with pressure group complaints in a positive way, more people may find themselves jumping on a pressure-group bandwagon, more administrators may find themselves bullied into removing materials arbitrarily from the schools and more teachers and librarians may be guilty of rejecting good materials because of the potential for controversy. One writer has stated:

> It is one thing to express honest criticism of some school text or teaching program and raise public questions about it. It is quite another to use group pressure to have certain materials banned because they do not conform to some special group's ideas about ... minority groups or whatnot. If we allow pressure groups rather than qualified educators to determine the content of school books, teaching in our schools will soon degenerate into indoctrination, with facts being embroiled with propaganda and truth tailored to fit some super-zealot's pet prejudice or theory (148, p. 202).

C. Teachers, Librarians and Administrators

One result of criticism and pressure may be that librarians and teachers are beginning to avoid materials that might be controversial even when they feel that these materials fulfil educational purposes.

At times the materials avoided by teachers have been approved by departments of education. In Manitoba schools, challenges to books approved by the Department of Education were becoming so frequent that the Manitoba Teachers' Society found it necessary to publicly state that it would support the right of teachers to use all books approved by the Department of Education. The Teachers' Society also recommended that teachers provide parents with advance information on new books that might encounter objections in order to explain their goals and avoid conflict situations (16).

Broderick (17) claims that secret removal of books by Canadian school administrators is not unheard of, while Fasick and England (122) suggests that younger librarians are more restrictive than older ones and engage in self-censorship to a greater degree.

Sometimes librarians, teachers, administrators or trustees are the ones who identify "objectionable" material. In Richmond, B.C., some trustees had *Go Ask Alice* removed from schools. Students submitted a 2,000-name petition against the banning and were supported by the Teacher-Librarians Association. One seventeen-year-old student stated, "I think by senior high school, we should have the right to read any book our teachers deem suitable for the classroom" (32). In spite of these objections, the school board transferred the books from the school to the local public library.

Opinion

Educators are human. They do, at times, make incorrect choices, misjudge needs, and use faulty methods. In short, they may need the input of parents, pressure groups and others. Broderick (17) cites an instance where a teacher assigned a book without reading it simply because multiple paperback copies were available. Following complaints from students to the vice-principal, and a reconsideration of the book by school personnel, another book replaced the one that had been questioned.

On the other hand, individuals and pressure groups must realize that parents ultimately have control only of their own children. If they succeed in restricting the reading material of children outside their own family, they must recognize that in so doing they are opening the door for any pressure group attempting to restrict the reading material of any children.

One of a number of criteria for selecting learning resources in the Vancouver School Board Policy statement states: "...learning resources shall be selected for their strengths rather than rejected for their weaknesses." Some censors focus their attention only on the weaknesses. Depending on how criticisms are made and how they are dealt with, they can serve to improve textbooks and selection policies.

Public meetings can assist parents and the community to understand the aims and methods of the school staff. Unfortunately, some criticisms inhibit an exchange of ideas and allow the opinions of one group to dominate. The line betweeen responding positively to a challenge and succumbing to censorship is very fine. Parents, teachers and administrators will require considerable sensitivity and integrity to deal with censorship issues in their communities. The very existence of a strong and viable education system is, in part, dependent on how conflicting viewpoints are handled and on how parents, educators and others respond to potentially volatile controversies over school books.

IV. How Are Challenged Materials Handled?

This chapter will describe the various ways in which challenged materials have been handled up to now. It is to be hoped that the recommendations that are made in the last chapter of this book will prevent temporary "solutions" from being relied upon in the future.

A. Deletions

One response to the problem of short or isolated offensive elements is to remove only the offensive parts of the book. Following one parent's complaint, a Winnipeg principal removed pictures of nudes from an art book (106). The leader of Renaissance International, Ken Campbell, has declared himself willing to edit Shakespeare and the Bible in order to make them acceptable for use with young children (74).

Following a complicated battle involving the Alberta Department of Education, the British Columbia Department of Education, the author of the story and many school boards, the publisher of a grade twelve anthology, *Story and Structure,* published a new edition with a number of offensive words deleted. The story in question, Philip Roth's "Defender of the Faith," was being used to illustrate characterization. The story had first appeared in *The New Yorker* magazine in 1959 without swear words but had been issued a year later in a collection of Roth stories, this time with swear words. Then an official version without swear words was published in September, 1966. Earlier in 1966, the publisher had already included the unedited version in *Story and Structure.* The British Columbia Department of Education authorized both old and new editions, and individual school boards decided which anthology their schools would use (3, 12, 54, 115). A third option was also available to school boards. The British Columbia Department of Education authorized schools to cross out the objectionable words in copies of the unedited books. An amusing account of this incident can be found in the article "Unsex me here ... you murd'ring ministers, or why the B-R-E-A-S-T stroke may be deleted from high school swimming courses." (54).

An incident mentioned in Chapter II centred on the anthology of short stories, *Impact*. The school solved its problem by physically taking the book apart, discarding the offensive story, "Debut", and using the remaining stories individually.

B. Restrictions on Usage

In Langley, B.C., an ad hoc committee of school librarians, parents and trustees recommended that the book *Go Ask Alice* be taken off library shelves and placed in counsellors' offices to be used at their discretion. However, the board decided to follow the lead of the Richmond, B.C., School Board by removing the book from the school setting (55). In Fort Garry, Manitoba, the book *Mao Tse Tung* was placed under restricted use. The book is still housed in the librarian's office and is available only to teachers or to elementary students with special permission. While there are probably many examples of this type of behaviour, such actions are rarely reported in the media.

C. Removal from the Curriculum

If a book is curriculum material, it may be dropped from the department of education approved reading list, or permission to teach the book may be withdrawn by the school board, super-intendent, or principal. The book may, however, be allowed to remain in the school library.

Mentioned in Chapter II is the B.C. incident in which the department of education removed the fairly new grade eight textbook *Strawberries and Other Secrets,* following complaints about episodes of violence and sexual characterizations (113). The details of this incident are outlined in figure 8.

In Peterborough, Ontario, a high school principal struck *Lives of Girls and Women* by Canadian author Alice Munro from the Grade 13 reading list in his school. The book remained in the school library. Because no formal procedures existed for handling complaints, the principal acted on his own initiative but found himself in the awkward position of having staff and students publicly criticize his action (98).

A Dufferin county education director was criticized by his colleagues because he removed *The Diviners* by Canadian author Margaret Laurence from the high school supplementary reading list even after a school board committee approved its inclusion. The director maintained that the removal was temporary, in order to give trustees time to read the book (13).

In the incident described in figure 13, the same book was removed from the high school curriculum in Peterborough county although a special committee had approved its inclusion. The subsequent debate continued for a year, with the school board voting in favour of retaining the book. As a result of the controversy, the book was left on the approved list, however, some teachers have avoided using it because of its potential for controversy.

Censorship of books in the curriculum is often "invisible", that is, it occurs at the moment of choosing one book over another. This kind of censorship does not make headlines, but some teachers are aware of the problem of "self-censorship" as described in Figure 12.

Figure 12:

Educators fear public criticism

SCHOOL TEXTS CENSORED TO AVERT CONTROVERSY

By Noelle Broughton

Many teachers and librarians are exercising self-censorship over controversial school books to avoid public backlash, according to some educators.

"There's self-censorship because no one likes to be bitten," said Levi Reimer, a former librarian who is now principal of Elmwood school in Altona.

Librarians and teachers "have always been very vulnerable to public criticism," said Manitoba Library Association president, Ron Friesen. He said this made them cautious when books became controversial.

Both Reimer and Friesen said this caution is reflected in policies of not ordering fiction books which might be controversial; placing sex and physiology books on a closed shelf, allowing only certain students to see them; or not teaching a controversial text book even though it's already in the school.

But the means used and the books censored depend on the community, said Reimer. Books considered controversial in one community may be acceptable in another.

Although such censorship may not be an "over-all major problem," Morden high school principal John Wiens said he believes every librarian experiences it to some degree.

Wiens said librarians may become more cautious after public outcries such as that in Virden, Man. last November. A community group there wanted books such as *All Quiet on the Western Front* and *To Kill a Mockingbird* banned from Virden's public high school.

Friesen suggested that every school division should have a policy for selecting books and handling public complaints to guard against "witch hunt situations" where librarians or teachers are confronted by a small community group.

Wiens said librarians and teachers would be protected by such a formal board policy because people would be deterred from making "frivolous complaints."

Reimer agreed that such a policy might provide teachers and librarians with a greater sense of job security. But he said it wouldn't necessarily help educators "hold their heads up in the community" after they've brought a controversial book into their school.

From "School texts censored to avert controversy" by Noelle Boughton,
WINNIPEG FREE PRESS, Feb. 7, 1979, p.3,
reprinted by permission of the WINNIPEG FREE PRESS.

Figure 13:

The Diviners Banned in Area High Schools

By Alan Toulin
Examiner Staff Writer

The Diviners, a best-selling novel by Lakefield author Margaret Laurence, has been banned from classrooms in Peterborough County.

The book was stricken from the curriculum although it had previously been approved as a text last year by the educational planning committee for use this year.

However, trustee Joe Hogan, chairman of a textbook review committee which examines material of a controversial nature, said he did not know the book was suspended.

Mr. Hogan said a committee under the auspices of the educational planning committee approves courses of study and texts for use in classrooms the year before they are to be used.

The committee has only the function of reviewing complaints about certain books because of content.

The committee is in the process of being restructured to give it a wider presentation said trustee Alicia Perry.

She said The Diviners, if it was in this year's texts for the English course in high schools, must have been approved for use.

"Someone obviously questioned it. If anyone does, it automatically is screened by the committee," she said.

Robert Buchanan, head of the English Department of Lakefield Secondary School, said he was told he could not teach the book in class, although it was on the course list and he had planned to teach it in May. Mr. Buchanan said the principal of the high school informed him the book had been stricken from the list of approved texts.

The English department head said the decision to ban the book was apparently an internal one made by the Peterborough County administration.

Director of Education for the county, Rae Linton, was unavailable for comment at press time. Joe Carey, head of the English department at PCVS, said the book has been banned across the county.

Mr. Carey said he recognized the rights of parents in the area of controversial books, but said "every single book we teach could offend somebody."

Miss Laurence said she was "extremely distressed and saddened" by the withdrawal of her book from the curriculum list.

"The reason is because the book has some four letter words and sexual scenes, but they are very necessary to the book," she said.

She described her work as a "profoundly religious book."

"It's about coming to terms with the past, with your ancestors, and a fiction about writing," she said.

The Lakefield novelist said the news was distressing, especially when high school English teachers have been trying to get more Canadian literature into the schools. In discussing her book with high school students, she said the students did not notice the language.

"I've talked to a lot of high school students and they have an intelligent perception of what the book is about," she said.

At a panel discussion held yesterday about book censorship, teachers expressed the view that self-censorship is being practised to avoid confrontations about the use of books as occurred last year when a group of parents successfully demanded the removal of the novel Flowers for Algernon.

This situation, said the teachers, detrimentally affected the education system.

Chairman of the review committee, Joe Hogan, said he could not comment on this view but he said the English teachers had an opportunity to appeal to his committee to get the book reinstated.

From "The Diviners Banned in Area High Schools"
by Alan Toulin, PETERBOROUGH EXAMINER, Feb. 7, 1976, p.1,
reprinted by permission of the PETERBOROUGH EXAMINER.

Figure 13: Something to think about

1. Who is responsible for curriculum content?
2. What should be the deciding factors in whether or not a book is suitable for compulsory curriculum content? For optional reading? For the school library?
3. What is/what should be the role of parents in decisions about curriculum content? Of teachers? Of the school administration? Of school boards? Of departments of education?
4. Margaret Laurence cites the opinions of high school students. Are the opinions of the students themselves significant? Why or why not?
5. In the panel discussion in Peterborough on self-censorship, the opinion was expressed that self-censorship which acts to soft-pedal issues that students are already aware of is a form of dishonesty. Is this a valid opinion? Why or why not?
6. Is it worth risking the formation of deep rifts in a community by using controversial materials in schools? Do the students learn anything from these controversies? In what way are these controversies detrimental to the educational system, as the Peterborough teachers say?

D. Banning

A book may be banned from the library as well as removed from the curriculum. Examples include the removal from the school library of *Sally Go Round the Sun* in Hamilton, Ontario (26), and *Anne Boleyn* in Port Credit, Ontario (Figure 9). In order to avoid "adverse publicity," a Toronto principal removed copies of *Peking Review* from the school library (142, p. 52)

A book banning may also be the result of a group complaint, as occurred when *The Diviners* was removed from both the curriculum and school libraries in Huron County (138, p. 51-55) and when *Go Ask Alice* was removed from a school in Langley, B.C. (55).

E. Firing

American journals cite instances of book bannings linked to teachers' losing their jobs, but only one instance of firing could be found in literature available to this author. In Moosomin, Saskatchewan, over a decade ago, a teacher was dismissed by the local board of education for "gross misconduct" when parents objected to her inclusion of the underground Vancouver newspaper

The Georgia Straight in classroom studies. The Saskatchewan Department of Education later ordered that the charge of "gross misconduct" be dropped, but the teacher was not reinstated at Moosomin (142, p. 13).

Perhaps the cry of "Fire the teacher" has not been heard more often because Canada has traditionally tended toward compromise rather than confrontation. However, with the heavy influence of American pressure group militancy in the area of school book censorship, the trend may be to move toward a win/lose conflict with a diminishing of the "Let's work together" mentality.

F. Full Access

Finally it appears that some educators and school adminstrators are less likely to remove materials or censor them than they were before censorship became a public issue. For example, in Western School District, Manitoba, a parent complained about the presence of *My Darling My Hamburger* in the high school library. The book deals with teenagers and the way they handle decisions about premarital sexual involvement and includes the problems faced by a girl who undergoes an abortion. After presenting an oral complaint, the parent was asked to present the complaint in writing to the school board. Following a reconsideration of the suitability of the book, the board allowed it to remain in the school library (77, 87).

At a York County (Ontario) Board of Education meeting, a motion to rescind approval of *Catcher in the Rye* and *The Apprenticeship of Duddy Kravitz* was defeated. Again, no books were banned. They remained on the approved curriculum list for senior secondary students (82).

An Elgin County, Ontario board chairman stated, "parents may review but not screen material" (88). In July, 1978, the Grey County, Ontario, Board of Education reversed its earlier decision to remove certain books from high school reading lists (138, p. 55). Following an emotional uproar in New Brunswick over "pornographic, obscene, profane and sexually exploitive language (in) school textbooks" (57), the curriculum committee firmly held their ground, stating that "books cannot be judged on individual words."

Examples cited in Figure 14 illustrate two ways in which school officials have learned to deal with censorship. The New Brunswick Department of Education reassured parents that no child would be forced to read anything to which his or her parents objected. The Kings County School Board, Nova Scotia, set up a selection policy and complaint form. No books were banned or removed.

Figure 14:

Censors lose two battles in Maritime provinces

Censorship doesn't win every round, as librarians in two Maritime provinces proved during a recent fight against banning books in some school libraries.

Through the spring of 1978, would-be censors in New Brunswick pressured the provincial department of education to remove some books they considered offensive. After extensive media coverage, the department issued a statement that no student would be forced to read anything to which his or her parents objected on moral or religious grounds. No change in policy took place and no books were removed from the libraries.

A similar censorship campaign later developed in Nova Scotia. Censors put the Kings County Amalgamated School Board under fire to remove some books and attempted to force a policy change in the department of education.

After refusing a request for an open meeting, the school board asked instead for written submissions from advisory committees and other interested groups. The Kings County School Library Association, among others, submitted a book selection policy complete with complaint form.

Eight months later, a brief book selection policy was adopted, and machinery set up for handling complaints. No written complaints have reached the board.

At the provincial level the department of education made diplomatic promises to one church group about exercising care in making new selections but did not ban any books.

From FELICITER, Oct, 1979, p.6, reproduced by permission of FELICITER.

Figure 14: Something to think about

1. Is the New Brunswick Department of Education statement that no student would be forced to read anything to which his or her parents objected a reasonable one? Why?
2. Did the Kings County Amalgamated School Board do the right thing in refusing the open meeting?
3. Is it fair to request complaints to be in writing? Will this requirement scare timid parents with legitimate concerns? What are the advantages of a written complaint over an oral one?

4. How significant is it that no complaints were made after selection policy and procedures for handling complaints were board-approved?
5. Is there any way of handling such situations without loaded words like "battles," "lose," "win," or "fight"?

Opinion

Given the spectrum of materials challenged, the intensity with which different persons attack or defend various school materials, the diverse ways in which criticism is met, and the variety of methods of dealing with challenged materials, it can be seen that issues relating to the selection of school materials are highly complex and sensitive. The crux of the problem rests in the pluralism of our society. If the "ghettoizing" of students into religious- or ethnic-based private schools is to be avoided, educators, parents, and interested individuals must find some satisfactory, acceptable and workable way of dealing with differences.

V. What Is Our Response?

The question of which materials best meet the educational requirements of individual students in particular regions across Canada is open to debate. All those involved in the censorship controversy seem to have different definitions of what is suitable. Obviously, not all materials are going to meet with the approval of all parents. How can parents deal with discrepancies between values taught at home and those dealt with at school? How can teachers and librarians feel free to use professional judgement in choosing good educational materials? How can administrators, school boards, trustees and departments of education ensure that good materials are chosen on the basis of merit without regard to potential controversy? How can concerned people respond constructively to the complex issue of controversial materials in our public schools? This chapter will deal with some possible, reasonable and constructive actions on the part of parents, teachers and librarians and administrators, school boards and departments of education.

A. Parents

Concerned parents should make personal and individual decisions regarding materials, without relying unduly on the opinions of others. The entire book, not just snippets, should be read: otherwise, the theme and full impact of the book can be obscured, and a knowledgeable dialogue with school personnel or children will be difficult, if not impossible. Gregory Clark, co-ordinator for the Writers' Federation of Nova Scotia, has said that quoting supposedly lewd passages out of context "has the effect of an obscene phone call" (110). Certainly, such quoting is not fair to the writer, the student, or the book. Figure 11 presents two ways in which snippets from *Catcher in the Rye* could be used to convey different points of view.

Keeping an open mind will help both parents and teachers to engage in dialogue. An emotional, hostile attitude on the part of a parent may have the effect of pushing the teacher into a defensive stance, where to change means to lose face. A hostile approach also places a child in the unfair position of having to choose between parent and teacher. Honest, rational communication may assist teachers to consider other viewpoints.

If parents get involved in the schooling of their children by going along on field trips, becoming active in the PTA and generally supporting the positive things the school is doing, not only will parents be more knowledgeable about the philosophy and total program of the school, but the teachers will probably be more informed and understanding of parental concerns.

It is wise for parents to discuss the material in question with their children before approaching the school or teacher. The discussion should be centred on the material itself, not on the teacher. If parents and children explore beliefs and opinions together, an interesting dialogue may develop, possibly strengthening family relationships.

Finally, if after an honest evaluation and an open discussion, a problem cannot be resolved, a formal, well thought out complaint should be presented to the school in writing.

B. Teachers and Librarians

It is imperative that teachers and librarians choose the best materials available and that they have a clearly thought out rationale for their choices. In order to articulate this rationale, it is necessary to have a wide knowledge of what is available. While a first-hand reading of all resource material is desirable, it is not always possible. Therefore, professional selection aids are often useful. The publications of departments of education and teachers' associations, library journals and annotated bibliographies are sources of selection information.* Curriculum and library book choices should be based on such criteria as suitability of subject matter, authenticity, scope, relevance, Canadian content and physical features. Availability, department of education guidelines, educational objectives and school board regulations must also be considered. Good materials should not be avoided because of their potential for controversy.

Teachers must consider concerns expressed by individual parents. If objections are raised, they should be seriously considered. Such

---

* *Publishers' catalogues are necessarily biased and do not make good selection aids.*

consideration may result in a program change for an individual child. Ideally, an open, rational dialogue, helping parent and teacher to understand each other better, would precede such action.

Finally, teachers must be firm in pressing for the development of written policies to handle challenged materials. Such policies can be effective in avoiding hasty or unwarranted actions, while making allowances for reasoned changes.

C. Administrators, School Boards and Departments of Education

The increased willingness on the part of some school boards to resist censorship attempts has been accompanied by a trend towards establishing procedures for dealing with challenged material. There are a number of reasons for establishing written guidelines for handling challenged material. First, guidelines provide a superintendent, principal, librarian or teacher with a defined course of action to follow when a dispute occurs. Educators will be less likely to remove challenged material by reflex reaction. Secondly, having a board-approved procedure increases the confidence of those directly involved when handling "touchy" issues. Thirdly, with duties and responsibilities clearly outlined, competency increases because school personnel know the procedure to be followed. Furthermore, members of the community who wish to raise a concern may feel more comfortable voicing their opinions through a known, accepted channel.

Selection committees, librarians and teachers do make errors. An acceptable, set procedure allows for changes to take place without any accompanying "loss of face".

Written procedures may also increase the community's support of the school, as people come to realize that the school has thought about the issue seriously and has allowed for input from concerned individuals. A procedure for facilitating dialogue in tense situations will assist parents, educators and others concerned about education in their attempts to communicate with each other.

Having a complaint procedure will not prevent pressure groups from forming. Procedures and guidelines may not rule out the appearance of hostility in the local press, may not prevent letters to the editor, may not always calm flaring tempers, and may not even result in the ideal co-operation between home and school. Written procedures for dealing with complaints will help to ensure that the best possible learning materials remain available to the majority of students, either through a reasoned removal of unsuitable material or through support of challenged material which meets selection criteria. Certainly, the existence of written criteria will prevent material from being removed from the reach of all students on the basis of one person's judgement or because of an emotional attack on the material.

Procedures for handling challenged material vary from school board to school board. Many have provisions for both formal and informal approaches to dealing with controversial materials. An informal approach is a necessary first step, which allows for a quiet, thoughtful acquaintance of school personnel with members of the community. However, if an informal exchange of ideas cannot solve the dilemma, it may be necessary to implement a formal procedure.

A formal complaint should be requested in writing. One school board supplies printed forms that can be used by people wishing to lodge a complaint against a book (see Appendix I for a sample form). The form should lead people to indicate whether the material has been read in its entirety, what the criticism is and what action they would like taken. A well-written rational complaint is more likely to cause teachers or librarians to reconsider their choice of material. Although they may still decide that the choice was a good one, they may be made aware of factors they had not considered.

Some policies suggest that the complaint be presented to the school principal and a notification be sent to the superintendent. A review committee, representing a spectrum of interests including parents, teachers, students, university professors, supervisors and others should be constituted. The composition of such a committee allows the issue to be discussed away from the emotions of a concerned parent or the defense mechanisms of a nervous teacher, librarian or principal, all of whom might be called upon to present their views, but who would not be members of the committee, thereby ensuring a fair hearing of the complaint.

One Canadian policy, which might be used as a model, is that of Vancouver School District #39, included in Appendix I. It includes a general statement of policy, procedures for handling informal complaints, and detailed procedures for handling formal complaints, including preliminary procedures, the composition and duties of the reconsideration committee, procedures for arriving at a resolution, and some general guiding principles.

For the same kinds of reasons that procedures for handling challenged materials should be worked out, policies of selection must be thought through and implemented. The survey in Appendix II illustrates that although some school boards are developing such policies, many school boards, even large-city systems, are still without such policies. In this survey no distinction is made between suggested guidelines and board-approved policies such as the Vancouver policy statement found in Appendix I. John Wilkinson's study found only 1.7 per cent of school libraries had written book selection policies (160, p. 60).

Various studies have shown the effects of selection policies in libraries. Pope's study (151) reveals that librarians working in institutions with written policies are less restrictive than those working elsewhere. Gerhardt (126) states that

> ...without a written agreement stating who is in charge of the library, the librarian's role in selection and collection management can be swept aside very quickly when a panicky principal responds to a parent's complaint, when any authoritarian superintendent of schools may, without discussion with principals and librarians, over-react to a single complaint or when group pressure threatens to engage in title-by-title quarrels over library book acquisitions.

She goes on to say that those working without such a policy, presuming that censorship situations will not occur, enjoy only foolish serenity." Olsen's study (133) reveals that public high schools with written policies explaining the procedures and criteria of selection are more successful in resolving censorship problems than high schools without such policies.

Textbooks and books in school libraries will always have faults. Authors are human and write from their own experiences and with their own prejudices. One of the tasks of professional educators is to identify those materials in which the strengths far outweigh the defects and to decide which materials can best meet educational objectives. The process of selection is too important for us to allow it to be governed by someone's whim.

School boards and departments of education must provide a clear statement of educational objectives and a policy on choosing materials to meet those objectives. In order for such a document to be of maximum use, it should be more than guidelines or suggestions, but should be a board-approved policy statement. A Nova Scotia Department of Education circular that was sent to various school board advisory committees in 1974 stated:

> Don't put off writing policy until book banners swamp or wreak havoc with your agenda. In the absence of a written policy many of your district's books may be tried not by law and professional educators but by headlines in your local press (110).

In writing such a policy, it is important to allow for a wide variety of types of reading materials. Nelson and Roberts in their study,

Censors and the Schools, state:

> Any sensible person would agree that there are risks involved in allowing young persons relatively free access to a wide range of reading material. Of course there are risks. But...there are greater risks in any alternative procedure. Surely we have not lost the courage to take risks that are necessary for the preservation of freedom (148).

Naturally, the criteria for selection, as well as the procedures discussed earlier for handling challenged materials, would be part of such a statement. Selection procedures for discarding out-of-date materials, accepting gifts, handling multiple sets, and selecting controversial materials should be stated.

A selection policy should also include a statement outlining the philosophy of the board's objectives. It is imperative to include a statement of who is responsible for selection. The Grey County Board of Education instructed its education director that "he must rule on all government-approved books before they [are] allowed into the schools" (100). The Manitoba Teachers' Society publicly upholds the teacher's right to use books authorized by the minister of education (116). The document should indicate where final authority resides. Is it vested in the department of education, the superintendent, the school board, the principal, or the individual librarian or teacher?

As previously mentioned, Vancouver School District #39 has a school board-approved selection policy which is included in Appendix I. It is an excellent statement of goals and has an impressive format which suggests the authority and importance of the identification of who is responsible for selection, the criteria for selection, specific procedures for selection, and procedures for handling challenged materials.

Opinion

This chapter has explored some ways of handling controversial school materials. Specific guidelines and suggestions concerning which books should be available to which students have not been considered. A definitive answer to that dilemma is impossible to give, not only because each child has different needs but also because each parent, teacher or other concerned person holds differing opinions. Furthermore, each community and each school has specific and distinct characteristics, which may call for the use of differing materials. The subject of censorship has been repeatedly discussed in many books and articles, and perhaps Gaines' statement that there is "only the slimmest possibility of anyone saying anything new on the subject" is a valid observation (125). However, as has been mentioned, one way of dealing with the problem is for schools to have a set of written procedures at their disposal, which will allow for the input of various and conflicting opinions.

In creating selection policies and procedures for handling challenged materials, educators must resist the urge to wave them about as clubs for self-protection. The purpose of such documents is to assist educators, parents and students to engage in dialogue. Policies should not be used to stifle complaints and questions but should help school personnel to respond positively to community concerns, parents to understand educational objectives and students to receive the best available materials. It is hoped that the current focus of the censors will shift from things "immoral, profane, seditious, heretical or otherwise offensive" to the positive and idealistic emphasis found in the quote from Philippians which opened this book. Energies now devoted to "banning" would then be turned to selecting and developing the best educational materials available.

Afterword

Finally, brethren
whatever is true,
whatever is honorable,
whatever is right,
whatever is pure,
whatever is lovely,
whatever is of good repute,
if there is any excellence, and
if anything worthy of praise,
let your mind dwell on these things.

The Bible
Philippians 4:8

An interpretation of this passage in terms of education might be that one must use the very best materials available in helping children and young adults to make the most of their lives. Even writers as far apart as Timothy Findley (46) and Paul Stuewe (108) would agree with this statement. Ideally, school districts across Canada will establish policies and procedures that allow for the existence and recognition of conflicting philosophies of life. As parents and educators of children, we must encourage a search for the truth of life (even if it means examining critically some areas in our own lives), demonstrate our knowledge of what's right with our actions even in crisis situations, take an honourable approach to children and young people in appreciating the pure and lovely (by giving them the example of our own appreciation for such things), place an emphasis on works of good repute (neither ignoring nor overstressing their short-comings), applaud excellence (wherever it manifests itself), help children to recognize and understand those things worthy of praise, (and identify those things unworthy of praise), and, all of us, parents, educators and children, must think on these things, calmly, and in the sincere desire to understand ourselves, those around us and ultimately the meaning of our place in the cosmos.

Appendix I

Selection
of Learning
Resources:

A Policy Statement

approved by the Board of School Trustees
of School District 39 (Vancouver)
on April 17, 1978

INTRODUCTION

At its meeting of April 17, 1978 the Board of School Trustees of School District 39 (Vancouver) approved unanimously this policy on the selection of learning resources. The statement is consistent with new provincial regulations and procedures on curriculum responsibility.

Part I of the document states the policy on the selection of learning resources, provides a definition of learning resources and outlines the objectives of selection, criteria to be applied, procedures to be followed, as well as responsibility for the selection program.

Part II states the policy for dealing with challenged materials and provides guidelines for both an informal and formal reconsideration of a learning resource, as well as guiding principles for a reconsideration committee.

This policy is designed to explain how learning resources are selected for use in Vancouver schools and to provide for consideration of the opinions of those persons in the school and community who are not directly involved in the selection process.

Selection Of Learning Resources:

I. STATEMENT OF POLICY

The policy of the Board of School Trustees of School District #39 (Vancouver) is to provide a wide range of learning resources at varying levels of difficulty, with diversity of appeal and the presentation of different points of view to meet the needs of students and teachers.

II. OBJECTIVES OF SELECTION

A. For the purposes of this statement of policy, the term "learning resources" will refer to any person(s) or any material (whether acquired or locally produced) with instructional content or function that is used for formal or informal teaching/learning purposes. Learning resources include textbooks, other books, supplementary reading and informational materials, charts, community resource people, agencies and organizations. dioramas, filmstrips, flash cards. games, globes, kits, machine readable data files, maps, microfilms, models. motion pictures, periodicals, pictures, realia, slides, sound recordings, transparencies and videorecords.

B. The primary objective of learning resources is to support, enrich and help to implement the educational program of the school through the interaction of professional personnel and other members of the school community. It is the duty of professional staff to provide students with a wide range of materials at varying levels of difficulty, with diversity of appeal and the presentation of different points of view.

C. To this end, the Board of School Trustees of School District #39 (Vancouver) affirms that it is the responsibility of its professional staff:
   — To provide materials that will enrich and support the curriculum, taking into consideration the varied interests. abilities, learning styles and maturity levels of the students served;
   — To provide materials that will stimulate growth in factual knowledge, literary appreciation, aesthetic values, and societal standards;
   — To provide materials on various sides of controversial issues so that young citizens may have an opportunity to develop under guidance the practice of critical analysis and to make informed judgements in their daily lives;
   — To provide materials representative of the many religious, ethnic, and cultural groups and their contributions to our national heritage and the world community;
   — To place principle above personal opinion and reason above prejudice in the selection of materials of the highest quality in order to assure a comprehensive collection appropriate to the school community.

III. RESPONSIBILITY FOR SELECTION OF LEARNING RESOURCES

A. The Board of School Trustees delegates the responsibility for the selection of learning resources to the professional staff employed by the school system.

B. While selection of learning resources involves many people (administrators, teachers, students, community persons, resource centre personnel) the responsibility for coordinating the selection of school learning resources and making the recommendation for purchase rests with the principal and professional personnel.

IV. CRITERIA FOR SELECTION OF LEARNING RESOURCES

A. The following criteria will be used as they apply:

   1. Learning resources shall support and be consistent with the general educational goals of the province and district and the aims and objectives of individual schools and specific courses.
   2. Learning resources shall meet high standards of quality in factual content and presentation.
   3. Learning resources shall be appropriate for the subject area and for the age, emotional development, ability level, learning styles and social development of the students for whom the materials are selected.
   4. Learning resources shall have aesthetic, literary, and/or social values.
   5. Physical format and appearance of learning resources shall be suitable for their intended use.
   6. Learning resources chosen shall be developed by competent authors and producers.
   7. Learning resources shall be designed to help students gain an awareness of our pluralistic society as well as an understanding of the many important contributions made to our civilization by women and minority and ethnic groups.
   8. Learning resources shall be designed to motivate students and staff to examine their own attitudes and behaviors and to comprehend their own duties, responsibilities, rights and privileges as participating citizens in our society.
   9. Learning resources shall be selected for their strengths rather than rejected for their weaknesses.
   10. Biased or slanted learning resources may be provided to meet specific curriculum objectives; for example, to recognize propaganda and its purpose in a given context or to balance an argument.

B. The selection of learning resources on controversial issues will be directed towards maintaining a balanced collection representing various views.
   Learning resources shall clarify historical and contemporary forces by presenting and analyzing intergroup tension and conflict objectively, placing emphasis on recognizing and understanding social and economic problems.

C. Emphasis will be placed on the selection of Canadian learning resources where appropriate. These resources include book and non-book learning materials by or about a Canadian person, about a region or event, and/or published or produced in Canada.

V. PROCEDURES FOR SELECTION OF LEARNING RESOURCES

A. In selecting learning resources, professional personnel will evaluate available resources and curriculum needs and will consult reputable, professionally prepared aids to selection and other appropriate sources. The actual resource will be examined whenever possible.

B. Recommendations for purchase involve administrators, teachers, students, district personnel and community persons, as appropriate.

C. Gift materials shall be judged by the criteria outlined and shall be accepted or rejected by those criteria.

D. Selection is an ongoing process which should include the removal of materials no longer appropriate and the replacement of lost and worn materials still of educational value.

Procedures For Dealing With Challenged Materials:

I. STATEMENT OF POLICY

Any resident or employee of the school district may formally challenge learning resources used in the district's educational program on the basis of appropriateness. This procedure is for the purpose of considering the opinions of those persons in the schools and the community who are not directly involved in the selection process.

II. REQUEST FOR INFORMAL RECONSIDERATION

A. The school receiving a complaint regarding a learning resource shall try to resolve the issue informally.

  1. The principal or other appropriate staff shall explain to the questioner the school's selection procedure, criteria, and qualifications of those persons selecting the resource.
  2. The principal or other appropriate staff shall explain the particular place the questioned resource occupies in the education program, its intended educational usefulness, and additional information regarding its use, or refer the party to someone who can identify and explain the use of the resource.
  3. If the questioner wishes to file a formal challenge, a copy of the district Selection of Learning Resources policy and a Request for Reconsideration of Learning Resources form shall be mailed by the principal to the party concerned.

III. REQUEST FOR FORMAL RECONSIDERATION

A. Preliminary Procedures

  1. Each school will keep on hand and make available Request for Reconsideration of Learning Resources forms. All formal objections to learning resources must be made on these forms.
  2. The Request for Reconsideration of Learning Resources form shall be signed by the questioner and filed with the principal or someone so designated by the principal.
  3. The area assistant superintendent and the assistant superintendent of curriculum services shall be informed of the formal complaint received.
  4. The request for reconsideration shall be referred to a reconsideration committee at the school level for re-evaluation of the resource.
  5. Requests for reconsideration of materials in district collections shall be referred to the school resource centre consultative committee for re-evaluation of the resource. This committee may involve additional personnel as appropriate.

B. The Reconsideration Committee

1. Upon receipt of a request for formal reconsideration of a learning resource, the principal is responsible for:

   a) Consulting with the chairpersons of the staff committee council, school consultative committee and student council regarding the composition of the school reconsideration committee;

   b) Forming the reconsideration committee. When appropriate, membership should include:
   — One member of the district staff chosen by the area assistant superintendent;
   — One member of the school teaching staff chosen by the school staff;
   — One member of the resource centre professional staff chosen by the resource centre professional staff;
   — One member of the school consultative committee chosen by the school consultative committee;
   — Two students chosen by the student body.

   c) Naming the convenor of the reconsideration committee;

   d) Establishing a meeting date as soon as possible after the complaint is received.

2. The reconsideration committee may choose to consult district support staff and/or community persons with related professional knowledge.

3. The reconsideration committee shall review the challenged resource and judge whether it conforms to the principles of selection outlined in the district's Selection of Learning Resources policy.

C. Resolution

1. The reconsideration committee shall proceed within these guidelines:

   a) Examine the challenged resource;
   b) Determine professional acceptance by reading critical reviews of the resource;
   c) Weight values and faults and form opinions based on the material as a whole rather than on passages or sections taken out of context;
   d) Discuss the challenged resource in the context of the educational program;
   e) Discuss the challenged item with the individual questioner when appropriate;
   f) Prepare a written report.

2. The written report shall be discussed with the individual questioner if requested.

3. The written report shall be retained by the school principal, with copies forwarded to the assistant superintendent of curriculum services and the area assistant superintendent. A minority report may also be filed.

4. Written reports, once filed, are confidential and available for examination by trustees and appropriate officials only.

5. The decision of the reconsideration committee is binding for the individual school.

6. Notwithstanding any procedure outlined in this policy, the questioner shall have the right to appeal any decision of the reconsideration committee to the Board of School Trustees as the final review panel.

D. **Guiding Principles**

1. Any resident or employee of the school district may raise objection to learning resources used in a school's educational program despite the fact that the individuals selecting such resources were duly qualified to make the selection, followed the proper procedure and observed the criteria for selecting learning resources.

2. The principal should review the selection and objection rules with the teaching staff at least annually. The staff should be reminded that the right to object to learning resources is one granted by policies enacted by the Board of School Trustees.

3. No parent has the right to determine reading, viewing or listening matter for students other than his/her own children.

4. Although it is the learning resources which are challenged, the principles of the freedom to read/listen/view must be defended as well.

5. Access to challenged material shall not be restricted during the reconsideration process.

6. The major criterion for the final decision is the appropriateness of the material for its intended educational use.

7. A decision to sustain a challenge shall not necessarily be interpreted as a judgement of irresponsibility on the part of the professionals involved in the original selection and/or use of the material.

VANCOUVER SCHOOL BOARD
REQUEST FOR RECONSIDERATION OF LEARNING RESOURCES

Initiated by _____

Telephone No _____ Address _____

Name of School _____

REPRESENTING

Self _____ Group (give name) _____

Organization (give name) _____

RESOURCE QUESTIONED

Book: Author _____

      Title _____

      Publisher _____

      Copyright Date _____

      Hardcover _____ or Paperback _____

Nonbook: Type of Resource _____
                         (Magazine, film, filmstrip, record, person, community resource, etc.)

      Title/Name _____

      Publisher or Producer _____

Please respond to the following questions; if sufficient space is not provided, feel free to use additional sheets of paper.

1. Did you review the entire item? _____ If not, what sections did you review? _____

_____

2. To what do you object? Please be specific. _____

_____

_____

_____

3. What do you believe is the main idea of this material? _____

_____

_____

4. What do you feel might be the result of a student using this material? _____

_____

_____

_____

5. Is there anything good about this material? _____

_____

_____

6. Are you aware of the judgement of this material by professional critics? _____

_____

7. In your opinion, for what age group would this material be more appropriate? _____

_____

8. In the place of this material, would you care to recommend other material that you consider to be more appropriate?

_____

_____

_____

_____

_____   _____
Date   Signed

Please return this form to the school principal.

Copies will be sent to the area assistant superintendent and the assistant superintendent of curriculum services.

From "Selection of Learning Resources", April 17, 1978 reproduced by permission of the Board of School Trustees of School District no.39 (Vancouver).

Appendix II

SELECTION POLICY STATEMENTS:
THEIR STATUS IN CANADIAN SCHOOL SYSTEMS

A Survey by Gerald Brown:
Chief Librarian, Winnipeg School Division No. 1

In March of 1978 a preliminary survey questionnaire was circulated to 320 Boards of Education across Canada. Both public and separate systems were included. Each board was invited to submit a copy of any existing selection policy statement and to indicate the authority of the endorsing agency. Cases where a policy was in the draft stage or where no policy existed were also identified.

A return rate of only 17.5 per cent over the following eighteen months caused serious concern, especially when a number of Boards with large enrolments had not reported.

In September of 1979 a second appeal was directed to the 36 largest city-based school boards as identified by the Canadian Education Association. In addition, a telephone follow-up was used to contact several Boards reported to have formal statements in the final stages of preparation. These second efforts to solicit examples of official policy statements boosted the returns to 23 or 63.8% of the 36 largest city-based boards and 76 or 23.4% of the overall Canadian survey, including replies of "no selection policy statement available at this time." Of the 36 largest city-based school boards, thirteen did not reply, fourteen submitted selection policy statements and nine responded with "no selection policy statement available at this time."

Based on the total survey response, the following lists designate which school boards or other agencies have, do not have or are preparing selection policy statements as of April, 1980.

RESPONDING SCHOOL BOARDS AND OTHER
EDUCATIONAL AGENCIES: SELECTION POLICY
STATEMENTS SUBMITTED

1. Bay of Islands — St. George's Integrated School Board, Nfld.
2. British Columbia School Library Assoc. B.C.

3. Centre de Documentation, La Commission Scolaire Regionale de l'Yamaska St.-Hyacinthe, Quebec.
4. Eugene Burdenuik, formerly of Timmins High and Vocational School, Timmins, Ont. (from *Moccasin Telegraph,* 18.3.15 —21, 1976.)
5. Coquitlam School District #43, B.C.
6. Dufferin-Peel Roman Catholic Separate School Board, Ont.
7. Durham Board of Education, Oshawa, Ont.
8. Drayton Senior Public School, Ont.
9. Edmonton Public School Board, Alta.
10. Fort Garry School Division, Man.
11. Halifax City School Board, Nova Scotia
12. John McCree Public School, Guelph, Ont.
13. Kings County Amalgamated School Board, Kentville, Nova Scotia
14. London Board of Education (Elementary), Ont.
15. Niagara South Board of Education, Ont.
16. North Island Regional School Board, Montreal, Quebec
17. North York Board of Education, Toronto, Ont.
18. Peterborough County Board of Education, Ont.
19. Port-au-Port Roman Catholic School Board, Stephenville, Nfld.
20. Red Deer School Board, Alta.
21. Regina Board of Education, Sask.
22. Rockwood Centennial School/Community Library, Ont.
23. St. Boniface School Division, Man.
24. St. Vital School Division, Man.
25. Saskatchewan Dept. of Education, Sask.
26. Saskatoon Board of Education, Sask (1977 + 79 rev.)
27. Scarborough Board of Education, Ont.
28. Toronto Metropolitan Separate School Board, Ont.
29. Vancouver School District, B.C.
30. Vernon School District, B.C.
31. Wellington County Board of Education, Ont.
32. Western School Division, Morden, Man.
33. Winnipeg School Division, Man.

No distinction made between board approved policy statements and suggested guidelines.

RESPONDING SCHOOL BOARDS AND OTHER EDUCATIONAL AGENCIES: NO SELECTION POLICY STATEMENT AVAILABLE (APRIL 1980)
1. Brandon S.D. Manitoba
2. Carleton Board of Education, Ottawa

3. Carleton R.C. School Board, Ottawa
4. Dartmouth S.D. Nova Scotia
5. Deer Lake Integrated School Board, Nfld.
6. East York Board of Education, Toronto
7. Etobicoke Board of Education, Ont.
8. Halton Board of Education, Ont.
9. Hamilton Board of Education, Ont.
10. Hastings-Prince Edward R.C.S.S.B. Trenton, Ont.
11. Hôpital Notre Dame, Montreal, Quebec
12. Howe Sound S.D. B.C.
13. Kamloops Learning Resource Centre, B.C.
14. Kamsack S. Unit #35, Sask.
15. Langley S.D. B.C.
16. Laurentian S.B. Lachine, Quebec
17. Lethbridge S.D. #51, Alta.
18. Medicine Hat S.D. #76, Alta.
19. Middlesex County Board of Education, Ontario
20. Mont Laurier Centre de Documentation, CSR Henri Bourassa, Quebec
21. Nanaimo S.D. #68, B.C.
22. Oxford County Board of Education, Woodstock, Ont.
23. Pentecostal Assemblies, Board of Education, Windsor, Nfld.
24. Protestant S.B. of Greater Montreal, Quebec.
25. River East S.D. Manitoba
26. Rosthern S. Unit #49, Sask.
27. Saanich S.D. #63, B.C.
28. St. Paul Regional School, St. Paul, Alta.
29. Saskatoon (West) S.D. Sask.
30. School District #34, Kindersley, Sask.
31. Sudbury Separate School Board, Ontario
32. Sydney School System, Nova Scotia
33. Terra Nova Integrated S.B. Nfld.
34. Timiskaming Board of Education, Ontario
35. Victoria S.D. B.C.
36. Wentworth County Board of Education, Ontario
37. York County Board of Education, Aurora, Ontario
38. Yorkton S. Unit #36, Sask.
39. Anonymous
40. Anonymous

RESPONDING SCHOOL BOARDS AND OTHER AGENCIES: SELECTION POLICY STATEMENTS IN PREPARATION (APRIL, 1980)

1. Albert-Westmorland-Kent Regional Library, N.B.

2. Assiniboine-South S.D. #3, Manitoba
3. London Board of Education (Secondary), Ontario

*From "Selection Policy Statements" by Gerald Brown, April 1980,
reprinted by permission of Gerald Brown.*

Appendix III
REPORT OF THE TASK FORCE
ON TEXTBOOK EVALUATION
TO THE HON. BEN HANUSCHAK,
MINISTER OF EDUCATION, MANITOBA

GUIDELINES TO MINIMIZE PREJUDICE AND BIAS IN TEXTBOOKS

Those general characteristics which are deemed to be desirable in the creation of textbooks designed to reduce prejudice and bias may be divided into various categories. We have, for convenience and ease of reference, divided this guide into two broad sections which include several categories.

I.   Historical Accuracy and Balance

   Concreteness and Inclusiveness

   1. a. Texts should identify the source of information wherever statements purport to be factual, in order to minimize editorializing, generalization, vagueness and ambiguity. In the event that original source material is unavailable, students should be made aware that the view presented is an interpretation of the facts.

   b. Where actual documents are available, reference should be made to them with special attention being given to presentation of different points of view, should these exist.

   2. Accounts of a particular event should clearly indicate that they reflect the perceptions, attitudes, language, concerns and setting of the times referred to.

   3. The subject matter should be dealt with in a balanced way in order to cover multiple aspects of the event or situation including the contributions of various people or groups of people and their popular or unpopular positions, different cultural approaches, controversial viewpoints, varying roles, and occupations.

   4. Subject matter specifically dealing with vocational and occupational roles should provide information about as wide a spectrum of opportunities available in society as is

possible, with specific care to avoid the presentation of sex-typed occupational categories.

II. Comprehensiveness and Unity

Language and Realism

5. In order to reduce the danger of attributing selected characteristics of an individual to the total group of which that person is a part, adjectives or phrases descriptive of the human character should relate to an identifiable person rather than to an identifiable group of persons.

6. Where a particular group of persons is described in an account, the information should be presented in a complete and meaningful way rather than in a fragmented or scattered fashion.

7. Pictures and illustrations should be congruent with the coverage allocated to the persons or events discussed, supported by an appropriate caption of the picture's location, time and date.

8. Slanting by way of value-loaded words or labels should be avoided.

9. Illustrations and written material must not perpetuate stereotypes about people based upon race, religion, creed, nationality, ancestry, ethnicity, sex, color, age, culture.

10. Social evils, including prejudice and discrimination, should be examined rather than ignored. Current and past events should receive frank and realistic treatment. Matters of broad social concern, whether regarded as negative or positive, should not be omitted or ignored but should be identified and explored.

11. Illustrations in texts should reflect the wide variety of individual differences within all segments of our society.

From the "Report of the Task Force on Textbook Evaluation
to the Hon. Ben Hanuschak, Minister of Education, Manitoba,"
Nov. 1976, p.8-9, reprinted by permission of the Manitoba Department of Education.

Appendix IV

GUIDELINES FOR ELIMINATING SEXISM IN READERS

We recommend that the following guidelines be considered by the Department of Education in conjunction with the Human Rights Commission when assessing readers for Nova Scotia schools. These recommendations should also be forwarded to publishers and authors for their use when preparing new material. If the following criteria are not met, the text in question should not be accepted by either the publisher or the school board.

1. Both girls and women should receive as much exposure in the readers as boys and men. This means there have to be many more stories and illustrations about females, thus eliminating male predominance.

2. People of both sexes and all age groups should be portrayed as having a variety of character traits, not just those traditionally considered appropriate for their sex. Girls and women should be assertive and independent, boys and men gentle and intuitive without implicit negative associations.

3. Both sexes should be engaged in a wide range of activities beyond those normally associated with each sex. For example, girls as well as boys should be involved in active sports and performing household tasks. Men should be cooks as well as mechanics, and women, woodworkers as well as seamstresses.

   Neither sex shown should be consistently portrayed as incompetently performing certain tasks. Both sexes should be shown successfully completing their tasks with equal frequency and each should receive positive social sanction as a result.

4. Women and men should be shown in positions of authority among their peers and children. Men as well as women should be shown caring for and directing children, while women should be shown capable of holding a position of authority in a job situation.

5. Alternative life styles for each sex and age group portrayed should be described within the context of stories. Single adults, childless couples, adopted children, divorced adults and orphaned children, to name a few, as well as married couples with children, should be depicted. The readers should include stories of people from all age groups, from babies to the elderly.

6. Clothing of both sexes should be appropriate for the activity. The stereotype of girls in dresses and bows while boys are in rough and ready playclothes should be avoided.

7. People of all ages should be involved in different groups. Boys should be shown with women as frequently as with men, and girls with men as frequently as with women. Further, adult women should be engaged in group activities among their own sex and with men as often as men are shown with men. Similarly, children of both sexes should be involved in peer group activities.

8. Factual material should be presented without reference to gender, or, where necessary, both sexes should be included. Sexist language should be replaced with non-sexist terms such as *human, you, I* or *one*.

9. Natural animal stories should avoid portraying the female as mother only, but involve her in various other activities as well. Conversely, the role of male as father should be included in the description of his pattern of behaviour.

10. Reference to appearance should be avoided when irrelevant. For example, girls and women should never be described in terms of their appearance while boys and men are praised for their abilities.

From "Sexism in School Textbooks"
by Judi Donahue, Janice Newton, and Peggy Simmie,
NOVA SCOTIA HUMAN RIGHTS COMMISSION, 1976, p.63-65,
reprinted by permission of the Nova Scotia Human Rights Commission.

Appendix V

FREEDOM FOR LEARNING: THE REPORT OF THE COMMITTEE ON ACADEMIC FREEDOM AND RESPONSIBILITY OF THE ONTARIO SECONDARY SCHOOL TEACHERS' FEDERATION

SOME HINTS FOR DEALING WITH A CENSORSHIP CAMPAIGN

These suggestions should be followed in areas where there are no formal school board policies, procedures, guidelines or understandings about how to react to censorship campaigns.

1. Stay calm. Beware of rash or poorly-considered actions.

2. Get in touch with the Professional Services Cluster at the Provincial OSSTF office. We have resources to help you.

3. Maintain effective links within your district/division and within your school. Communicate closely with your district/division OSSTF and senior administration. Be sure that full, accurate information about every aspect of the problem is available for all concerned teachers.

4. Don't try to establish long-range policies or procedures at the height of a censorship campaign; be very cautious. Don't rush through ineffective or flawed policies and procedures.

5. Enlist as much "local help" as you can. There may be groups or organizations in your community who sympathize with you.

6. Document everything that happens. Try to get the position of the various parties involved, including your board and senior administration, in writing if you can. Provide your local district or division office and the Provincial Office with copies.

7. Deal with the issue in a professionally responsible manner. Don't retreat into bureaucratic solidarity and indifference as a means of defense.

8. Help is available, but you will have to commit yourself to a potentially tough struggle. The principles involved are vital to the teaching profession and we must defend them professionally and with commitment.

WORKING WITH THE SCHOOL COMMUNITY

The modern public secondary school provides its services for a great variety of individuals who come from a variety of home situations. Some students are sophisticated beyond their years, others are quite naive; some homes provide negligible moral guidance for their children, others are insistent that the "highest moral standards" of the home are not only respected by, but also implemented in the school.

When extreme viewpoints are brought to bear on books, films, and other instructional materials, an emotional confrontation between parents and the school often follows. Public challenges may then take place, with charges such as "moral pollution" and "censorship" being voiced. Such consequences are not likely to prove profitable for anyone.

As professionals we should be discriminating in the selection of educational materials. This process of selection should arise from a teacher's conscientious adherence to professional, educational criteria, not from censorship imposed by external groups or individuals. This is the kind of accountability to self imposed by any caring teacher who wants to provide for the needs of each student in the most effective way possible.

How can the school and the teacher carry out this process in a positive, effective way?

Some Suggestions

- be sensitive to and respectful of the attitudes of individuals in each class, and of the wishes of their parents.
- take every reasonable opportunity to inform parents of the detail of course content and material, and give them the opportunity to examine these items. This can be done with great positive effect during Parents' Nights, Program Nights, Open House and Visitation Days.
- be aware of the general standards of morality which prevail in the school community.
- choose books and other materials which are appropriate for the age group and social maturity of the student.
- provided the course objectives are not compromised, consider non-controversial as well as potentially controversial materials.
- it goes without saying that no book, film, or other material should be used which has not been thoroughly read or examined by the teachers concerned. Teachers, department heads, and principals must be prepared to discuss their instructional materials with

parents, and to explain the context in which the material is used and how it relates to the objectives of the course.

- after informing students that material to be used in class may contain elements which could be offensive to some, the teacher must be prepared to allow individual students to select optional topics of study. Furthermore, this choice must be made with discretion so as not to cause embarrassment to anyone.

- teachers are human. Be prepared to admit that a mistake has been made where such an admission is warranted.

- a formalized process should be available to allow complaints to be brought to the board of education. It is suggested that an objective, non-threatening form might be used to facilitate the collection of specific information about the nature of the complaint.

Many confrontations may be avoided or defused when teachers are ready to accept parental concerns or complaints as a normal situation. Being "ready" means that teachers have used good judgement in choosing materials, and have shown sensitivity and respect for the feelings of each student and the opinions of parents.

From "Freedom for Learning: The Report of the Committee on Academic Freedom and Responsibility", ONTARIO SECONDARY SCHOOL TEACHERS' FEDERATION, 1981, p.6-8, reprinted by permission of the Ontario Secondary School Teachers' Federation.

BIBLIOGRAPHY

Magazine and newspaper articles about cases of censorship in Canada

1. Adachi, Ken. "Censors under attack." *Toronto Star,* January 12, 1979, p. B1.

2. Allan, Ted. "Brief attacks prejudiced school texts." *Winnipeg Tribune,* April 23, 1969, p. 13.

3. "Aw. fff-forget it, U.S. author says." *Vancouver Sun,* November 2, 1967, p. 1.

4. Ayre, John. "Bill, book and scandal." *Weekend Magazine,* August 28, 1976.

5. "Banned book back." *Vancouver Province,* January 7, 1970, p. 11.

6. "Battle of books shaping in East." *Winnipeg Tribune,* January 18, 1979, p. 37.

7. Barkman, Alma. "Blowing too hard." *Carillon News,* March 5, 1980.

8. Barth, Lloyd. "The Diviners: the road to destruction." *Orbit,* vol. 10, no. 4, October, 1979, p. 5.

9. Bateson, Helen. "A rewrite of the roles." *Vancouver Province,* March 8, 1974, p. 30.

10. Beissel, Henry. "Battling the book banners." *Quill & Quire,* vol. 45, no. 2, February, 1979, p. 6, 13.

11. Birks, Nancy. "Parents seek voice in choice of books." *Winnipeg Free Press,* June 23, 1977, p. 28.

12. "Board keeps nose clean in issue of dirty word." *Vancouver Sun,* November 21, 1967, p. 14.

13. Book is ordered off Dufferin school list." *Globe and Mail,* June 21, 1976, p. 9.

14. Boughton, Noelle. "Can parents ban books?" *Winnipeg Free Press,* October 3, 1978, p. 1.

15. Boughton, Noelle. "School texts censored to avert controversy." *Winnipeg Free Press,* February 7, 1979, p. 3.

16. Boughton, Noelle. "Teacher's right to use book okayed by Ministry upheld." *Winnipeg Free Press,* March 30, 1979, p. 12.

17. Broderick, Dorothy. "Censorship — Canadian style." *Moccasin Telegraph,* vol. 18, no. 3, Fall, 1976, p. 6-11.

18. "Burn books: brief." *Winnipeg Free Press,* April 12, 1978.

19. Callwood, June. "Obscenity and the Writers' Union of Canada." *CAUT Bulletin,* vol. 25, no. 11, October, 1978, p. 11.

20. Callwood, June. "Reason not passion." *Books in Canada,* November, 1979, p. 6.

21. "Canadian novels too sexy for classroom study." *Quill & Quire,* vol. 42, no. 3, 1976, p. 1.

22. "Censors lose two battles in Maritime provinces." *Feliciter,* vol. 25, no. 10, October, 1979, p. 6.

23. "Censorship." *Quill & Quire,* vol. 26, no. 2, April, 1960, p. 10.

24. "Censorship: th* b**k b*nn*rs." *Canada and the World,* vol. 45, January, 1980, p. 7-8.

25. Chatelin, Ray. "All-Russians-are-bad textbook faces ban here." *Vancouver Province,* October 18, 1972, p. 1.

26. "Children's book withdrawn from school." *Quill & Quire,* January, 1973, p. 6.

27. "Cleaning book shelves." *The Winnipeg Sun,* November 28, 1980, p. 6.

28. Cohen, Ruth. "Plan to ban unread books 'contemptible'." Letter. *Globe and Mail,* January 20, 1979, p. 7.

29. Connel, Helen. "Book battle hot in Huron County." *Halifax Chronicle Herald,* January 19, 1979, p. 7.

30. "Councillor cries fie at 'Catcher in Rye'." *Globe and Mail,* February 7, 1963, p. 5.

31. Dagg, Michael. "Regulation threatens librarians' integrity." *Feliciter,* February, 1978, p. 12.

32. Daniels, Alan. "Students want Alice back on shelf." *Vancouver Sun,* February 11, 1978, p. B6.

33. Davidson, Heather. "Wolfville board seeking opinion." *Halifax Chronicle Herald,* March 25, 1978, p. 17.

34. Douglas, L. Letter. *Globe and Mail,* January 20, 1979, p. 7.

35. Dowhan, Lynn. "Book censorship election issue." *Brandon Sun,* October 20, 1978.

36. Dowhan, Lynn. "Fort La Bosse candidate defends school textbooks." *Brandon Sun,* October 25, 1978.

37. Dowhan, Lynn. "Some progress made on Virden controversy." *Brandon Sun,* December 1, 1978.

38. Dowhan, Lynn. "Superintendent opposes book censorship." *Brandon Sun,* October 21, 1978.

39. Dowhan, Lynn. "Virden meeting set on book issue." *Brandon Sun,* November 23, 1978.

40. Downey, W. "The dangers of censoring books in our society." *Winnipeg Tribune,* July 21, 1978, p. 9.

41. Doyle, Mary Ellen. "Renaissance calls for free choice in our society." Letter. *Winnipeg Tribune,* May 3, 1977, p. 9.

42. Drabble, John. "Pastor protests 'immoral' book." *Winnipeg Tribune,* February 3, 1978, p. 3.

43. Duffield, Verna. "Censorship not the issue in textbook controversy." *Brandon Sun,* November 30, 1978.

44. Etherington, Virginia. "School reading list to be sent to parents." *Toronto Star,* June 28, 1979.

45. Farquharson, W. John. "Censors needed to contain flood of filth, salaciousness." Letter. *Winnipeg Tribune,* August 3, 1978, p. 9.

46. Findley, Timothy. "Better dead that read? An opposing view." *Books in Canada,* October 1978, p. 3-5.

47. Findley, Timothy. "Let's call it regimentation of culture." *Update,* vol. 20, no. 2, November 1978, p. 11.

48. Fluxgold, Howard. "Trustees change their opinion after they read banned books." *Globe and Mail,* June 12, 1980, p. 5.

49. French, William. "Banding together against bans." *Globe and Mail,* January 16, 1979, p. 13.

50. French, William. "The Good Book versus good books." *Globe and Mail,* June 14, 1978, p. 9.

51. Friesen, Ralph. Letter. *Carillon News,* March 12, 1980.

52. Friesen, Ron. "Beware of self-appointed censors." *Manitoba Library Association Bulletin,* vol. 9, no. 2, March, 1979, p. 13.

53. Geist, T. Letter. *Globe and Mail,* January 20, 1979, p. 7.

54. Gibson, Stan. "Unsex me here...you murd'ring ministers or Why the B-R-E-A-S-T stroke may be deleted from high school swimming courses." *Monday Morning,* vol. 4, no. 2, October, 1969, p. 22-23.

55. "Go Ask Alice banished from Langley schools." *Vancouver Sun,* February 9, 1978, p. C9.

56. "Grey County trustees bring you 1984 — now." *Toronto Star,* January 21, 1979, p. F4.

57. Hall, Stephen. "Sound and fury — book banners ride again." *ACT,* vol. 1, January, 1979, p. 16-20.

58. Haverluck, Tim. "Book ban request to be investigated." *Winnipeg Free Press,* June 1, 1978, p. 71.

59. Hudson, Robert. "Parents can't ban books." Letter. *Winnipeg Free Press,* October 16, 1978, p. 42.

60. Hussey, Valerie. Letter. *Globe and Mail,* January 20, 1979, p. 7.

61. "Indian yarn splits school board." *Victoria Times,* June 1, 1972, p. 10.

62. "Indians also slam reader." *Victoria Times,* June 14, 1972, p. 7.

63. Jones, Frank. "Book bannings. Order. Smugness. How one town swung to the right." *Toronto Star,* January 21, 1979, p. A3.

64. Kamieusk. "Brave New World." Cartoon. *Winnipeg Tribune,* November 29, 1978, p. 8.

65. Kean, J.M. "Censorship, sexism and racism." *Arizona English Bulletin,* February, 1975, p. 59-63.

66. Kenny, L.M. and J.R. Blackburn. "Textbooks." Letter. *Globe and Mail,* November 2, 1976, p. 6.

67. Lavoie, T. "Obscenity in the classroom." Letter. *Winnipeg Tribune,* November 25, 1978, p. 9.

68. Lewis, Terry. Letter. *Carillon News,* February 27, 1980.

69. Lipovenko, Dorothy. "Book about Christ's death angers North York parents." *Globe and Mail,* November 17, 1978, p. 4.

70. Lowndes, Colin. Letter. *Books in Canada,* vol. 8, January, 1979, p. 24-25.

71. Marrus, Michael R. "Textbooks." Letter. *Globe and Mail,* November 10, 1976, p. 4.

72. Marshall, John. "Persuasion needed to beat book bans, teacher told." *Globe and Mail,* November 5, 1979, p. 11.

73. McGarry, Michael. "School text rapped." *Winnipeg Tribune,* January 25, 1969, p. 34.

74. McGrath, Joan. "Intellectual freedom and Canadian libraries." *In Review,* vol. 13, no. 6, December, 1979, p. 10-13.

75. McKinley, Patrick. "Censor group won't take part." *Winnipeg Tribune,* November 28, 1978, p. 12.

76. McNaught, Kenneth. "Censoring history texts supine surrender: historian." *Globe and Mail,* October 30, 1976, p. 7.

77. "My Darling, My Hamburger goes back on the shelf." *Dufferin Leader,* March 31, 1976, p. 40.

78. "Mysterious case of forbidden fruit." *Update,* vol. 20, no. 3, December, 1978, p. 6-7.

79. "N.S. Home and School to discuss censorship." *Halifax Chronicle Herald,* June 13, 1978, p. 21.

80. Neufeld, Moira. "Local educator upset over Renaissance ad." *Carillon News,* February 27, 1980.

81. Neufeld, Wayne and Moira. Letter. *Carillon News,* March 12, 1980.

82. "No ban on books." *Ontario Education,* vol. 8, no. 5, November, 1976, p. 5.

83. "No garbage literature in schools, Cosens says." *Brandon Sun,* November 7, 1978.

84. Nowlan, Michael. "Book banning takes evangelistic twist." *Quill & Quire,* August, 1978, p. 33.

85. "Ontario parents request review of school books." *School Library Journal,* vol. 25, September, 1978, p. 14.

86. Parker, Graham. Letter. *Books in Canada,* vol. 8, January 1979, p. 24-25.

87. "Parent expresses objection to school library book." *Manitoba School Library Audio Visual Association Journal,* vol. 3, no. 4, May, 1976, p. 39.

88. "Parents advocate censorship of books." *Quill & Quire,* July, 1978, p. 33.

89. "Pentecostals critical of textbooks, teachers in tax-supported schools." *Portage La Prairie Daily Graphic,* August 30, 1978.

90. Peterson, Leslie. "Censorship on the rise." *Vancouver Sun,* February 22, 1980, p. 21.

91. Potter, Sheldon. Letter. *Winnipeg Tribune,* March 18, 1977, p. 9.

92. Riedner, Loretta. "Should school reading material be same as corner drugstore?" Letter. *Winnipeg Tribune,* May 19, 1977, p. 9.

93. Rivers, Margaret. "Book banners deprive students." *Orbit,* vol. 10, no. 4, October, 1979, p. 7.

94. Robertson, Jo. "Censorship a virtue?" *Halifax Chronicle Herald,* April 28, 1978, p. 7.

95. "'Russia' textbook withdrawn." *Vancouver Province,* October 19, 1972, p. 1.

96. "Sadistic savage school reader to be dropped by book publisher." *Globe and Mail,* April 20, 1976, p. 10.

97. Sadler, Joan. "Once upon a time once exciting." *Winnipeg Tribune,* February 7, 1978, p. 4.

98. Sallot, Jeff. "Students overwhelmingly against high school principal who opposes Munro novel." *Globe and Mail,* February 14, 1976, p. 3.

99. Sanders, H.A. Letter. *Globe and Mail,* January 20, 1979, p. 7.

100. "School board to have veto over choice of English texts." *Globe and Mail,* January 16, 1979, p. 1.

101. "School books anger parents." *Winnipeg Tribune,* June 21, 1977, p. 4.

102. "School text purge bid nonsense, says official." *Vancouver Sun,* October 27, 1969, p. 25.

103. "Scrubbing okayed." *Vancouver Sun,* November 14, 1967, p. 2.

104. " 'Sexism' adviser not a book burner." *Vancouver Sun,* September 3, 1974, p. 20.

105. Shaw, Russ. "Waskada parents settle textbook controversy." *Brandon Sun,* October 23, 1978.

106. Smith, Chris and Susan Janz. "New school books carefully screened." *Winnipeg Tribune,* June 22, 1977, p. 1.

107. " 'Socialist junk' unsold." *Winnipeg Free Press,* June 14, 1979, p. 7.

108. Stuewe, Paul. "Better dead than read." *Books in Canada,* October, 1978, p. 3-5.

109. "Subliminally anti-Semitic book covers to be removed." *Globe and Mail,* November 17, 1978, p. 4.

110. Surette, Ralph. "Censor group after school books." *Globe and Mail,* April 29, 1978, p. 8.

111. Sutherland, Duane. "Forum." *Education Today,* vol. 4, no. 9, June 1978, p. 2.

112. "Teachers self-censors?" *Peterborough Examiner,* February 7, 1976, p. 1.

113. "Textbook withdrawn." *Winnipeg Tribune,* December 2, 1978, p. 94.

113a. Toulin, Alan. "The Diviners Banned in Area High Schools." *Peterborough Examiner,* February 7, 1976, p. 1.

114. "Trustees ban The Diviners in Huron schools." *Globe and Mail,* August 22, 1978, p. 9.

115. "Trustees object to story." *Vancouver Sun,* October 25, 1967, p. 53.

116. Wayda, Diane. "Writers unite to fight censorship." *Winnipeg Free Press,* February 16, 1979, p. 29.

117. "Writers challenge censors." *Feliciter,* vol. 25, no. 12, December, 1979, p. 4.

General journal articles

118. Buress, Lee. "Pressure of censorship on Wisconsin schools." *Wisconsin English Journal,* October 1, 1963, p. 6-19.

119. Busha, Charles H. "Intellectual freedom and censorship: the climate of opinion in midwestern public libraries." *Library Quarterly,* vol. 42, no. 3, July, 1972, p. 283-301.

120. Cavanagh, Gray and Ken Styles. "The many faces of censorship." *Canadian Library Journal,* vol. 38, no. 3, June, 1981, pp. 123-132.

121. Dilliard, Irving. "Censorship and the freedom to read." *Illinois Libraries,* vol. 47, May, 1965, p. 449-455.

122. Fasick, Adele and Claire England. "Evaluating controversial materials for children and young adults." *Canadian Library Journal,* vol. 37, no. 1, February 1980, p. 29-34.

123. Fraser, J. "The Circular 14 story: approved textbooks in Ontario." *Orbit,* vol. 10, no. 4, October, 1979, p. 8-9.

124. Friesen, Ron. "Waiting for the censor." *Manitoba School Library Audio Visual Association Journal,* vol. 4, no. 1, September, 1976, p. 4-6.

125. Gaines, Ervin. "The dangers of censorship." *American Library Association Bulletin,* vol. 58, 1964, p. 595-596.

126. Gerhardt, Lillian. "Who's in charge of schools? *School Library Journal,* vol. 23, November, 1976, p. 27-28.

127. Jenkinson, David. "Profile: Keith Wilson." *In Review,* vol. 14, December, 1980, pp. 19-22.

128. Lorimer, James. "The political economy of Canadian publishing." *This Magazine,* vol. 9, no. 3, 1975, p.

129. Martin, Eva. "Services for children and young adults in the eighties." *In Review,* vol. 14, no. 5, October 1980, p. 5-11.

130. McCormack, Thelma. "Passionate protests: feminists and censorship." *Canadian Forum,* vol. 59, March, 1980, p. 5-8.

131. Naylor, David. "Censorship in our schools: the need for a democratic perspective." *Social Education,* vol, 42, no. 2, February, 1978, p. 118-121.

132. Neil, S.D. "Censorship and the uncertain librarian." *Canadian Library Journal,* vol. 32, no. 6, October, 1975, p. 345-348.

133. Olsen, Turee. "Censorship and selection." *Journal of Reading,* vol 17, March, 1974, p. 502-503.

134. Shugert, Diane. "What beginning English teachers need to know about censorship." *English Education,* vol. 10, May, 1979, p. 237-240.

135. Taxel, Joel. "Justice and cultural conflict: racism, sexism and instructional materials." *Interchange,* vol. 9, no. 1, 1978-79, p. 56-84.

136. Tomey, Pat. "Coping with censorship: a practical primer for school librarians." *In Review,* vol. 13, no. 6, December, 1979, p. 14-17.

Books, Reports and Pamphlets

137. Atnikov, Pamela, Irma Oleson and Glen McRuer. *A Study of Social Studies Textbooks Approved for Use in Manitoba.* Human Rights Commission, 1971.

138. Birdsall, Peter and Delores Broten. *MindWar: Book Censorship in English Canada.* Victoria: CanLit, 1978.

139. Campbell, Ken. *Christian Liberation.* Pamphlet produced in co-operation with Renaissance, 1978.

140. Campbell, Ken. *Tempest in a Teapot.* Cambridge: Coronation, 1975.

141. Donahue, Judi, Janice Newton and Peggy Simmie. *Sexism in School Textbooks.* Nova Scotia Human Rights Commission, 1976.

142. Eisenberg, John and Gailand MacQueen. *Don't Teach That.* Markham: Paperjacks, 1972.

143. Fiske, Marjorie. *Book Selection and Censorship.* Berkeley: University of California, 1968.

144. *Improving the Image of Women in Textbooks.* Scott, Foresman, 1974.

145. Katz, Edward. "The reactions of students from four Manitoba high schools to potentially controversial passages in English literature courses." Unpublished research paper. University of Manitoba, 1977.

146. Lewis, Terry. Renaissance Manitoba. "Education in Manitoba: New Problems and Changing Perspectives." Brief Presented to St. Vital School Division. Winnipeg, April 14, 1977.

147. Merritt, LeRoy Charles. *Book Selection and Intellectual Freedom.* H.W. Wilson, 1970.

148. Nelson, Jack and Gene Roberts. *The Censors and the Schools.* Boston: Little, Brown, 1963.

149. Ontario Status of Women. *About Face: Toward a More Positive Image of Women in Textbooks.* 1975.

150. Osborne, Kenneth. *The Image of the Worker in Canadian Social Studies Textbooks.* University of Manitoba Educational Foundation, 1980.

151. Pope, Michael. *Sex and the Undecided Librarian.* Metuchen: Scarecrow, 1974.

151a. *"The Rape of Children's Minds."* Interim Report no. 2, Ad Hoc Committee Respecting the Status of Women in the North York System, 1975.

152. Renaissance Manitoba. Newsletter. December 1976.

152a. Renaissance Manitoba. Newsletter. February 1979.

153. Report of the Task Force on Textbook Evaluation to the Honourable Ben Hanuschak, Minister of Education, Manitoba. November, 1976.

154. *A Response to the Royal Commission on Book Publishing.* Canadian Book Publishers' Council. Toronto, 1973.

155. Riel, Arthur. *Contrasting Views on Censorship.* ERIC Processing and Reference Facility: Bethesda, 1977. ED 145 474.

156. Robinson, Paul. *Where Our Survival Lies: Students and Textbooks in Atlantic Canada.* Atlantic Institute of Education, 1979.

157. *Selection of Learning Resources: A Policy Statement.* School Trustees of School District 39 (Vancouver). British Columbia, April 17, 1978.

158. *The Shocking Truth About Indians in Textbooks.* Manitoba Indian Brotherhood, 1977.

159. Stamp, Robert. *About Schools: What Every Parent Should Know.* New Press, 1975.

160. Wilkinson, John. *Canadian Juvenile Fiction and the Library Market.* Canadian Library Association, 1976.

161. Women for Non-Sexist Education. *Confronting the Stereotypes: Handbook on Bias at the Primary Level.* Manitoba Human Rights Commission and Department of Education, 1977.

162. Work Groups on Educational and Library Materials. *Canadian Books in Canadian Schools: A Case Study.* Association of Canadian Publishers, 1977.

163. Writers' Union of Canada. *C*ns*rsh*p: Stopping the Book Banners.* Toronto: Book and Periodical Development Council, 1978.

ACKNOWLEDGEMENTS

I wish to thank David Jenkinson, who inspired the writing of this work, who read several drafts and who made many valuable suggestions. His probing questions, gentle criticism and tactful advice had a strong impact on the format and content of this book.

I am grateful to the Manitoba Teachers' Society, which funded some of my initial research.

I appreciate the many articles, selection policies and other materials sent to me by numerous people, including Gerald Brown and Moira Neufeld. The service of the interlibrary loan department at the University of Manitoba was invaluable.

Finally, I must thank my husband, Harold, whose patience and encouragement were a necessary support.